The UK Juice Industry

Profiles of the leading 330 companies

John D Blackburn

Editor

dp

First Edition

Spring 2019

ISBN-13: 978-1-912736-16-4

ISBN-10: 1-912736-16-0

All rights reserved. No part of this publication may be reproduced, distributed, or transmitted in any form or by any means, including photocopying, recording, or other electronic or mechanical methods, without our prior written permission, except in the case of brief quotations embodied in critical reviews and certain other non-commercial uses permitted by copyright law. For permission requests, please write to us.

Copyright © 2019 Dellam Publishing Limited

Printed in 8pt Nimbus Sans L

Designed by URW++ Design and Development GmbH

Dellam Publishing Limited

2 Heath Drive, Sutton, Surrey, SM2 5RP

Fax: 020 8770 7478   email: enquiries@dellam.com

SAN: 0177881   EAN/GLN: 5030670177882

Table of Contents

1 Acknowledgements iv

2 Introduction v

3 Total Assets League Table 1
- As a measure of size, total assets is preferable to turnover which is influenced by profit margins and whether companies are capital or labour intensive.

4 Age of Companies 3
- Each company is ranked by its date of incorporation. Newcomers are defined as those registered since 2017.

5 Geographic Distribution 7
- Each company is classed by county.

6 Company Profiles 11
- Full company name, date incorporated, net worth, total assets, registered office, activities, shareholders and parent company, directors (with date of birth, nationality and occupation) and number of employees (if available).

7 Index of Directorships 31
- Alphabetical list of directors showing their directorships. If several directors have identical names then their date of birth is shown.

8 Standard Industrial Classification 39
- These codes are used to classify businesses by the type of economic activity in which they are engaged.

9 *finis* 43

Acknowledgements

This is a long and detailed publication containing thousands of facts and figures. It is only to be expected, despite continuous and repeated editing and checking, that errors may occur. In such cases, once we are aware of any, we publish a correction on our website.

Readers are encouraged to check regularly at www.dellam.com/books for any corrections and updates.

Although we take extreme care to ensure accuracy and being up-to-date, we cannot accept responsibility for any errors or omissions.

Contains public sector information licensed under Open Government Licence v3.0. from The Charity Commission (England and Wales) and The Charity Commission for Northern Ireland. © Crown Copyright and database right (2018).

Contains information from the Scottish Charity Register supplied by the Office of the Scottish Charity Regulator and licensed under the Open Government Licence v.2.0. © Crown Copyright and database right (2018).

Contains OS data © Crown copyright and database right (2018)

Contains Royal Mail data © Royal Mail copyright and database right (2018)

Contains National Statistics data © Crown copyright and database right (2018)

Contains Office for National Statistics © Crown copyright and database right (2018)

Maps based on those produced by the Office for National Statistics Geography GIS & Mapping Unit (2012 and 2018).

Contains HM Land Registry data © Crown copyright and database right (2018).

Contains Parliamentary information licensed under the Open Parliament Licence v3.0.

House of Commons Library Briefing Papers licensed under the Open Parliament Licence v3.0.

Contains Food Standards Agency data © Crown copyright and database right (2018).

Contains Eurostat data, 1995-2018, copyright European Commission by the Decision of 12 December 2011.

Maps based on produced by ONS Geography GIS & Mapping Unit.

Contains Companies House data supplied under section 47 and 50 of the Copyright, Designs and Patents Act 1988 and Schedule 1 of the Database Regulations (SI 1997/3032).

We appreciate your interest in our publications, and your comments and suggestions are always welcome. Please contact us at enquiries@dellam.com.

Introduction

This study looks at all companies registered in the United Kingdom where they identify themselves as manufacturers of fruit and vegetable juice.

This study includes companies that are dormant or non-trading some of which might be latent while others may operate under their owners' names but incorporate to protect the business name. In addition, all newly incorporated companies are included. The study will exclude those companies that do not specifically identify themselves as manufacturers of fruit and vegetable juice.

The aim of this study is to provide an overview of the key movers and shakers in the UK fruit and vegetable juice sector. Only key data has been isolated, particularly the company's net worth and total assets, but also its full name, date incorporated, registered office, other activities, shareholders, directors (with date of birth, occupation and nationality) and number of employees.

Two indicators of size are used: net worth and total assets. These are preferable to turnover which is influenced by profit margins and whether the companies are capital or labour intensive.

In the years 2016, 2017 and 2018, new company incorporations in the fruit and vegetable juice sector were 31, 49 and 102 respectively. The UK accounts for 19% of the European juice market.

The British Fruit Juice Association (BFJA) represents the industry in the UK.

The market for bottled water and fruit juice, neither of which contain added sugar, is unaffected by the sugar levy but nonetheless they do contain naturally-occurring sugars. Despite their natural sugar content, sales of freshly squeezed juices are increasing with smoothies the fastest growing segment. Own label sales are not at a disadvantage to branded products.

100% juice is the most important factor in choosing a product. For healthy soft drinks, consumers look at sugar content, then calories, whether it is natural and whether it is fresh.

Breakdown of beverages in the UK is as follows: soft drinks (28%), beer (27%), whisky (25%), cider (7%), gin (3%), mineral water (3%) and others (2%).

The breadown for non-alcoholic sector is as follows: cola £1.2 billion; pure juice £851 million; juice drinks £429 million; smoothies £223 million; plain water £616 million; squashes £406 million; traditional mixers £192 million; and fruit carbonates £405 million.

In terms of Gross Value Added (GVA) beverages (including soft drinks and mineral water) is the largest manufacturing group with a of £6.6 billion in 2015; contributing 23% to the total food and drink manufacturing GVA. The percentage UK retail price increase from June 2007 to June 2016 for soft drinks was 24% with alcoholic drinks at 17% and coffee, tea, cocoa at 36%

In Great Britain, 57% of those aged 16 years and over in 2017 drank alcohol (29 million people of the population) while 20% did not drink alcohol at all. Meantime there has been an increase in the number of juice bars.

Standard cataloguing guidelines for company names in the profile section have been used, but there will be occurrences when the name may not be strictly alphabetical. A certain licence was adopted where it was felt that strictly alphabetical could lead to improper cataloguing. Some company names have been shortened in the league tables for aesthetic reasons.

John D Blackburn
Editor

This page is intentionally left blank

Total Assets League Table

Company	Amount	Company	Amount
Baxters Food Group Limited	£305,020,992	Handmade Cider Company Limited	£40,447
Innocent Limited	£121,799,000	Juice A Day Limited	£39,529
Alpro (UK) Limited	£81,150,000	Lytegro Limited	£32,102
Fresh Trading Limited	£49,264,000	Presse Limited	£31,885
Orchard House Foods Limited	£47,484,000	Analytical-Solutions UK Ltd	£27,473
Fruitapeel (Juice) Ltd	£11,136,089	The Pickle House Limited	£26,646
Sundance Partners Limited	£6,418,852	H & D Ventures Limited	£24,557
Juiceworks Limited	£3,600,311	Barsupply Limited	£23,902
Asher & Son (Fruit & Vegetable Supplies) Limited	£3,231,579	Garden Press Ltd	£23,381
Benburb Bramleys Limited	£2,657,777	PAS Engineering Limited	£22,154
Pixley Berries (Juice) Limited	£2,325,956	Alkalize Me Ltd	£21,708
Duskin Farm Limited	£2,032,433	E & M Soroka Ltd	£21,345
Coldpress Foods Limited	£1,861,154	Realdrink Ltd	£20,605
Plenish Cleanse Ltd	£1,647,191	The Cotswold Fruit Company Ltd.	£17,607
Tower Nursery Limited	£1,526,129	Oliviccio Ltd	£13,683
Good Natured (Happy Monkey) Ltd	£1,221,809	Frugo Smoothies Ltd	£13,136
CPJLondon Ltd	£780,051	Pura Pressed Ltd	£12,334
Coton Orchard Limited	£681,787	Alba of Tonbridge Limited	£12,299
F. A. Young Farm Produce Limited	£647,309	Demcar UK Limited	£10,348
Waterperry Gardens Limited	£600,026	CCM Enterprises Limited	£10,025
Bensons Fruit Juice Limited	£590,317	Healthy Thirst Drinks Limited	£8,966
Juicebaby Ltd.	£532,755	Rosehip Farms Limited	£7,673
Ella Drinks Limited	£470,776	Juicee Beets Ltd	£7,232
Food Development Company Limited	£416,502	Love Yourself UK Limited	£6,600
Four Elms Fruit Farm Limited	£401,940	Wasted Apple Co Ltd	£5,265
Sunrise Produce Ltd	£352,030	Get Juiced (UK) Ltd	£4,809
TJ & PJ Dobson Ltd	£342,145	Devon Orchard Ltd	£3,503
Zendegii Retail Limited	£339,792	Fruitful Durham Community Interest Company	£3,143
CPRESS One Limited	£314,298	Zip & Zing Juices Ltd	£2,676
Livewheatgrass Limited	£305,562	Juices on the Go Ltd	£2,378
Bradleys Juices Limited	£283,747	Vegishake Ltd	£2,292
The Juice Smith Limited	£256,644	Natvitanet Ltd	£2,255
Zendegii Frill Limited	£256,393	Juice Philosophy Limited	£2,083
The Juice Executive Ltd	£234,227	Juice Fit JQ Limited	£1,848
The Simply Great Drinks (Europe) Limited	£219,396	Gerries Fruit Limited	£1,742
One54 Holdings Ltd	£216,819	Hero Solutions Limited	£1,328
H & R Partners Limited	£196,745	Lemony Drinks Ltd	£1,059
Four Elms Juice Limited	£180,193	Adunni Foods Ltd	£956
Rhythm Health Limited	£172,171	The Holy Grain Company Ltd.	£904
Liberty Orchards Limited	£169,754	Mobie Corporation Limited	£800
Ultimate Juice Limited	£164,090	Crown of Life Juices Ltd	£661
Trim and Trendy Limited	£142,870	Neema Food Ltd	£633
Gold Star Soft Drinks Westcountry Limited	£129,558	The Juicing Company Limited	£599
Andrew M Jarvis Limited	£90,669	Restore Juice Company Limited	£530
Grace Under Pressure Ltd	£89,890	Akiki Organics (UK) Limited	£455
Ben Crossman Limited	£87,091	Razoo Limited	£292
Passion 4 Juice Limited	£86,265	Impressive Juices Ltd	£262
Tiddly Pommes Ltd	£80,733	J.C.Davies & Hall Limited	£250
Elgin's Orchard Ltd	£71,662	AMM Ventures Ltd	£237
Chiltern Ridge Apple Juice Limited	£63,194	Smartervites Ltd	£100
Who Knows Limited	£60,582	Verjuice Limited	£100
Ipure Nutrition Limited	£56,968	Suppers Ready Limited	£5
ABA Foods Limited	£55,545	Wonky Food Limited	£3
Garden House Farms Limited	£54,340	Martina Peters Ltd	£1
Thornton Nurseries Ltd	£48,945	The Naked Juice Company Ltd	£1
Beermats4u Limited	£48,605	Spider Cider Ltd	£1
Onion Jo Limited	£46,040		

Age of Companies

1940-1949
Baxters Food Group Limited

1960-1969
Duskin Farm Limited

1970-1979
Asher & Son (Fruit & Vegetable Supplies)

1980-1989
Benburb Bramleys Limited
Orchard House Foods Limited
SVZ (UK) Limited
Waterperry Gardens Limited

1990-1994
Healthy Thirst Drinks Limited

1995
Coton Orchard Limited

1998
Ella Drinks Limited

1999
Alpro (UK) Limited
Fresh Trading Limited

2000
Innocent Limited

2002 [5]
Bensons Fruit Juice Limited
Four Elms Fruit Farm Limited
Juiceworks Limited
PAS Engineering Limited
Stamford Juice Co Ltd

2003
Passion 4 Juice Limited

2004
Elmsfield Enterprises Limited
Garden House Farms Limited
Trim and Trendy Limited

2005
Ben Crossman Limited
Direct Ingredients Limited
Ingredients Direct (UK) Ltd

2006
Alba of Tonbridge Limited
TJ & PJ Dobson Ltd

2007 [6]
Analytical-Solutions UK Ltd
Good Natured (Happy Monkey) Ltd
Oliviccio Ltd
Pixley Berries (Juice) Limited
Sinful Foods Limited
F. A. Young Farm Produce Ltd

2008
Sundance Partners Limited

2009 [8]
Endurance Juice Co Ltd
Food Development Co Ltd
Fresh Appeal Limited
Fruit Smoothies Ltd
Gold Star Soft Drinks Westcountry Ltd
Livewheatgrass Limited
Realdrink Ltd
Sunrise Produce Ltd

January-June 2010
Felukka Limited
Handmade Cider Co Ltd
Liberty Orchards Limited

July-December 2010
Frozen Cocktail Co Ltd
Gerries Fruit Limited
Who Knows Limited

January-June 2011
Little Stour Orchard Ltd
Thornton Nurseries Ltd

July-December 2011
Adunni Foods Ltd
Chiltern Ridge Apple Juice Ltd
Coldpress Foods Limited

January-March 2012
Zion Kitchen Limited

April-June 2012
Clearly Juice Limited
Plenish Cleanse Ltd

July-September 2012
Bradleys Juices Limited
California Girl Foods Ltd
Fruitful Durham CIC

October-December 2012
Zendegii Retail Limited

January-March 2013
Andrew M Jarvis Limited
Juicebaby Ltd.
Mobie Corporation Limited

April-June 2013
PG Foods Ltd
Pome de Vita Limited

July-September 2013
Spnet Ltd.

October-December 2013
ABA Foods Limited
Crown of Life Juices Ltd
Juice Garden Limited
Tower Nursery Limited

January-March 2014 [10]
Cowdray Live Ltd.
Devon Orchard Ltd
Ipure Nutrition Limited
Juice Fit JQ Limited
Juice Philosophy Limited
Juice Smith Limited
Rhythm Health Limited
E & M Soroka Ltd
Urban Juice Ltd
Zendegii Frill Limited

April-June 2014 [6]
CPRESS One Limited
Four Elms Juice Limited
Juice Executive Ltd
Martina Peters Ltd
Simply Great Drinks (Europe) Ltd
Suppers Ready Limited

July-September 2014
Ariana Foods (PVT) Ltd
Fruitapeel (Juice) Ltd
Get Juiced (UK) Ltd
Grace Under Pressure Ltd

October-December 2014 [6]
Cotswold Fruit Co Ltd.
Onion Jo Limited
Orchard Origins C.I.C.
That Healthy Way Limited
Wasted Apple Co Ltd
What's Good Limited

January 2015
Juices on the Go Ltd
Wonky Food Limited

February 2015
Karma Juice Ltd

March 2015 [5]
Beermats4u Limited
Chocquers Limited
Demcar UK Limited
Naked Juice Co Ltd
Smartervites Ltd

April 2015
Green-Beam Life Limited
Lytegro Limited
Raw Cure Limited

May 2015
Impressive Juices Ltd

July 2015
Holy Grain Co Ltd.
Natvitanet Ltd
Razoo Limited
Verjuice Limited

August 2015
MG International Trading UK Ltd

September 2015
Love Yourself UK Limited
Neema Food Ltd
One54 Holdings Ltd
Vegishake Ltd

October 2015
Umoba Ltd

November 2015
AMM Ventures Ltd
CCM Enterprises Limited
Funtime Products Limited
Spider Cider Ltd

December 2015
Hijama Ruqya Remedies Ltd
Trove International Limited

January 2016
Affybale Ltd
H & R Partners Limited
Pura Pressed Ltd
Zip & Zing Juices Ltd

February 2016 [5]
A2A Foods Limited
Aspire Better Health Limited
Carbon Fresh Limited
Nourish Juice Ltd
SRAM & MRAM Limited

March 2016
Restore Juice Co Ltd

May 2016
Bear & Organics Limited
Juice 1st Limited
Ultimate Juice Limited

June 2016
Barsupply Limited
Fimivita Agrimining Limited
Rose and Gold Drinks Limited

July 2016 [5]
Aero Cosmetics Limited
Garden Press Ltd
Juice A Day Limited
Lemony Drinks Ltd
Ready Steady Glow London Ltd

August 2016
Pure Press Ltd

September 2016
Frugo Smoothies Ltd

October 2016 [5]
Akiki Organics (UK) Limited
Ammo Your Ammunition to Greatness
Hero Solutions Limited
Juicee Beets Ltd
Tiddly Pommes Ltd

November 2016
Alkalize Me Ltd

December 2016
CPJLondon Ltd
SRAM & MRAM Technologies and Resources

January 2017
Avobravo Limited
J.C.Davies & Hall Limited
Greenie's Smoothies Limited
Kemetic Cooks Ltd

February 2017
Califia Farms UK Limited
Hunterworth Ltd

March 2017
H & D Ventures Limited
Juicing Co Ltd

April 2017 [6]
Brew Crew & Co. Limited
J.P Hinds Limited
JBC Juices Limited
Presse Limited
Rawness Limited
Rejuce Limited

May 2017
Armagh Juice Co Ltd
Clynes Farms Ltd
UK Dorset Ltd

June 2017
Borderless Catering Ltd
Eye Adom Market Limited
Real Shhh Limited

August 2017 [7]
Claense Ltd
Dnajuices Limited
Elgin's Orchard Ltd
Perfect Brands (Europe) Ltd
Pickle House Limited
Revive Us Limited
Wonky Group Ltd

September 2017
Degarnix Ltd
Perfect Brands Ltd
Rosehip Farms Limited
Smoofeez Limited

October 2017
Dean Press Cider Ltd.
Juice Junkiez Limited
Route 33 Limited
Sprosen Accounts Ltd

November 2017 [5]
Fitness Fruits Limited
Fresh Bagels Ltd.
Honestly Limited
Ice N Creamz Limited
Juice Junkie London Limited

December 2017 [9]
Bimim Foods Limited
Food and Drink Development Co Ltd
Go Fresh Ltd
Livitus Limited
Mebifarm Ltd
Purer Ltd
Vitsuk Ltd
Wild Cane Ltd.
Wise Herb Co Ltd

January 2018 [5]
Devon Garden Foods Limited
Go Super You Limited
Golden Hibiscus Foods and Drinks Ltd
Hainan Super Industrial Ltd
Judge Juice Ltd

February 2018 [9]
BSP Juice Ltd
Berrybegood Ltd
Bringing Eden Ltd
Cafe Tani Limited
Crosby Beverages Ltd
Healthy Drinks & Smoothie Ltd
Pastel D'Nata Ltd.
Proper Protein Co Ltd.
Suda Green REV Investment Ltd

March 2018 [13]
Cane Press Ltd
Chakra Chai Limited
Coco Twist Ltd
Cowherds Juicery Limited
Desert Raw Ltd
Juice and Go Ltd
Love Skin Co Ltd
Naturally Ugly Ltd
Neptune SA Ltd
Never Not Natural Ltd
Raw Candy Ltd
Sweet Palm Ltd
Truth Tonics Limited

April 2018 [11]
9 Pillars Ltd
Afgdryfruites.co.uk Limited
Anglo African Food & Beverages Holding
Azalizo Foods Ltd
Bear Dough Limited
Dboost Drinks Limited
DrJuicy Ltd
Get Fresh Ltd
Hibitala UK Limited
Karrmancooks Ltd
Phoenexus Ltd

May 2018 [7]
Doromomo & Sons Ltd
Fruit and Veg Co Leeds Ltd
J.T Freshly Limited
My Monkey Doesn't Like Bananas Anymore
Oxford Juice Co Ltd
Rafiq Costcutter Limited
Rejuveu Ltd

June 2018 [5]
AMC Freshly Squeezed (UK) Ltd
Agro Plus Limited
Exclusively Unique Ltd
Frol Explorer Ltd
Vegan Monster Ltd

July 2018 [10]
Ayad Corporation Ltd
Chefs Food Products Ltd
Frozenbeep Ltd
Glotedragon Ltd
Good MLK Ltd
Juice Tap Ltd
Juiced Ltd
Kleos Naturals Ltd
Orchard Blossoms Limited
Selva Group Limited

August 2018 [16]
Abanability Ltd
Dr. Chocolate Limited
Fruit International Limited
Health Hut NW Ltd
Islandgal Juice Ltd
Jamcan Ltd
Juice Delivery Service Ltd
Juice HQ Ltd
Juice Unit Ltd
Juice and Vegan Ltd
Odopa Foods Ltd
Olives Britannia Foreign Trade Co. Ltd
Sunlife Organics Limited
Tam Events & Cafe Ltd
Wellbeing and Balance Limited
Woolfies Ltd

September 2018 [7]
BB & F Consultants Limited

Gilt & Flint Ltd
Juice Freaks Co Ltd
LB Londom Ltd
LSG PVT Ltd
Little Teapot Ltd
Prickly Pear Potion Ltd

October 2018 [10]
Academic Fruits Limited
Drinks Group Holdings Ltd
Earthstrong Juicery Ltd
Ethically Made Ltd
FruitFullFruits Ltd
Iorange UK Limited
Pressed Ltd
Rootyfruit Limited
Snowdonia Birch Water Ltd
Wilanow:Import Export Ltd

November 2018
AWA Nature Ltd
Bare Goodness Limited
Dirty Milkshake Ltd
Neacsu Construct Ltd

December 2018 [5]
Dzatafia Ltd
Good Juice Co Ltd
Juicyology Ltd
McBerries Ltd
Seabuckthorn Scotland CIC

January 2019 [16]
AW Consultancy & Solutions Ltd
Amaze Offers Ltd
Bennu Rising Ltd.
Fruitfullest Ltd.
Fruiture Ltd
Get Juiced Tooting Ltd
H2T Food & Drink Limited
Hidden Orchard Ltd
Inside Armour Ltd
Kunubu Ltd
My Goodness (British Farmers) Ltd
Nattyroots Ital Juice Limited
Straight Up Zesty Ltd.
Strive Products Sco Limited
W & W Drinks Ltd
Watt (W) Ltd

February 2019 [10]
Bright Smoothies Ltd
Chakra Shots Limited
Fresh Manchester Ltd
Freshleigh Ltd
Juice Warrior Ltd
Muscle in Motion Ltd
Natural CBD Solutions Ltd
Purity Organic Juice Ltd
Rayner and Rooster Limited
Refreshing Drinks Co Ltd

Geographic Distribution by County

Co Armagh
Armagh Juice Co Ltd

Co Tyrone
Benburb Bramleys Limited

Aberdeenshire
Juicing Co Ltd

Angus
Ella Drinks Limited

Dumfries-shire
PAS Engineering Limited

Lanarkshire
Strive Products Sco Limited
Who Knows Limited

Moray
Elgin's Orchard Ltd

Stirlingshire
SRAM & MRAM Technologies and Resources

Bedfordshire
Alba of Tonbridge Limited
Trim and Trendy Limited

Berkshire [7]
Ammo Your Ammunition to Greatness
Berrybegood Ltd
Food and Drink Development Co Ltd
Karma Juice Ltd
Smartervites Ltd
W & W Drinks Ltd
Wise Herb Co Ltd

Buckinghamshire
Chiltern Ridge Apple Juice Ltd
Pome de Vita Limited
Tower Nursery Limited

Cambridgeshire
Coton Orchard Limited
Rayner and Rooster Limited

Cheshire [6]
Bear & Organics Limited
Dboost Drinks Limited
TJ & PJ Dobson Ltd
Fruit Smoothies Ltd
Garden Press Ltd
Ipure Nutrition Limited

Co Durham
Frozen Cocktail Co Ltd
Fruitful Durham CIC

Cornwall
Aero Cosmetics Limited
Hidden Orchard Ltd
Pura Pressed Ltd
Wasted Apple Co Ltd

Cumbria
McBerries Ltd

Derbyshire
Nattyroots Ital Juice Limited
Smoofeez Limited

Devon [8]
Devon Garden Foods Limited
Devon Orchard Ltd
Four Elms Fruit Farm Limited
Four Elms Juice Limited
Gilt & Flint Ltd
Gold Star Soft Drinks Westcountry Ltd
Onion Jo Limited
Realdrink Ltd

Dorset
Judge Juice Ltd
Liberty Orchards Limited

Essex [13]
A2A Foods Limited
Ethically Made Ltd
Freshleigh Ltd
Good Juice Co Ltd
Good Natured (Happy Monkey) Ltd
Greenie's Smoothies Limited
Iorange UK Limited
Juice HQ Ltd
Juice Philosophy Limited
Juiced Ltd
Lemony Drinks Ltd
Neptune SA Ltd
Umoba Ltd

Glamorgan [5]
Abanability Ltd
Degarnix Ltd
Fruitapeel (Juice) Ltd
H2T Food & Drink Limited
Healthy Drinks & Smoothie Ltd

Gloucestershire [6]
Bensons Fruit Juice Limited
Cotswold Fruit Co Ltd.
Passion 4 Juice Limited
Rosehip Farms Limited
Suppers Ready Limited
Woolfies Ltd

Gwent
Spider Cider Ltd

Gwynedd
Snowdonia Birch Water Ltd

Hampshire
Pastel D'Nata Ltd.
Revive Us Limited

Herefordshire
J.C.Davies & Hall Limited
Orchard Origins C.I.C.
Pixley Berries (Juice) Limited

Hertfordshire
Analytical-Solutions UK Ltd
CPJLondon Ltd
Gerries Fruit Limited
That Healthy Way Limited

Kent [16]
9 Pillars Ltd
Agro Plus Limited
Aspire Better Health Limited
California Girl Foods Ltd
Clearly Juice Limited
Crown of Life Juices Ltd
Doromomo & Sons Ltd
Duskin Farm Limited
Elmsfield Enterprises Limited
Jamcan Ltd
Juice Executive Ltd
Little Stour Orchard Ltd
My Goodness (British Farmers) Ltd
Raw Cure Limited
Rhythm Health Limited
Wild Cane Ltd.

Lancashire [20]
AMC Freshly Squeezed (UK) Ltd
Adunni Foods Ltd
Bear Dough Limited
Cowherds Juicery Limited
Fresh Manchester Ltd
Frozenbeep Ltd
Frugo Smoothies Ltd
Health Hut NW Ltd
Juicee Beets Ltd
Juiceworks Limited
Little Teapot Ltd
Naked Juice Co Ltd
Natural CBD Solutions Ltd
Odopa Foods Ltd
Oliviccio Ltd
Phoenexus Ltd
Proper Protein Co Ltd.
Purity Organic Juice Ltd
Rafiq Costcutter Limited
E & M Soroka Ltd

Leicestershire [5]
Coco Twist Ltd
Hibitala UK Limited
Lytegro Limited
Sinful Foods Limited
Thornton Nurseries Ltd

Lincolnshire
Fresh Appeal Limited
Stamford Juice Co Ltd

The UK Juice Industry

London [113]
ABA Foods Limited
AMM Ventures Ltd
AW Consultancy & Solutions Ltd
AWA Nature Ltd
Affybale Ltd
Alkalize Me Ltd
Amaze Offers Ltd
Anglo African Food & Beverages Holding
Asher & Son (Fruit & Vegetable Supplies)
Avobravo Limited
Ayad Corporation Ltd
Azalizo Foods Ltd
BB & F Consultants Limited
BSP Juice Ltd
Bare Goodness Limited
Barsupply Limited
Beermats4u Limited
Borderless Catering Ltd
Bringing Eden Ltd
CCM Enterprises Limited
Cafe Tani Limited
Califia Farms UK Limited
Cane Press Ltd
Carbon Fresh Limited
Chakra Chai Limited
Chakra Shots Limited
Chefs Food Products Ltd
Claense Ltd
Crosby Beverages Ltd
Demcar UK Limited
Dirty Milkshake Ltd
Dnajuices Limited
DrJuicy Ltd
Dzatafia Ltd
Endurance Juice Co Ltd
Fresh Bagels Ltd.
Fresh Trading Limited
Frol Explorer Ltd
FruitFullFruits Ltd
Fruitfullest Ltd.
Funtime Products Limited
Get Juiced Tooting Ltd
Go Fresh Ltd
Golden Hibiscus Foods and Drinks Ltd
Good MLK Ltd
H & R Partners LImlted
Hainan Super Industrial Ltd
Hero Solutions Limited
J.P Hinds Limited
Holy Grain Co Ltd.
Honestly Limited
Hunterworth Ltd
Ice N Creamz Limited
Innocent Limited
Islandgal Juice Ltd
JBC Juices Limited
Juice Junkie London Limited
Juice Junkiez Limited
Juice Tap Ltd
Juice Unit Ltd
Juice Warrior Ltd
Juice and Go Ltd
Juice and Vegan Ltd
Juicebaby Ltd.
Juices on the Go Ltd
Kemetic Cooks Ltd
Kleos Naturals Ltd
LSG PVT Ltd
Love Skin Co Ltd
Love Yourself UK Limited
MG International Trading UK Ltd
Mebifarm Ltd
Mobie Corporation Limited
Muscle in Motion Ltd
My Monkey Doesn't Like Bananas Anymore
Neacsu Construct Ltd
Neema Food Ltd
Olives Britannia Foreign Trade Co. Ltd
One54 Holdings Ltd
Orchard Blossoms Limited
PG Foods Ltd
Martina Peters Ltd
Pickle House Limited
Plenish Cleanse Ltd
Presse Limited
Prickly Pear Potion Ltd
Razoo Limited
Ready Steady Glow London Ltd
Real Shhh Limited
Refreshing Drinks Co Ltd
Rejuce Limited
Rejuveu Ltd
Rose and Gold Drinks Limited
Route 33 Limited
SRAM & MRAM Limited
Selva Group Limited
Sprosen Accounts Ltd
Straight Up Zesty Ltd.
Suda Green REV Investment Ltd
Sundance Partners Limited
Sweet Palm Ltd
Trove International Limited
UK Dorset Ltd
Urban Juice Ltd
Vegishake Ltd
Vitsuk Ltd
Watt (W) Ltd
What's Good Limited
Wilanow:Import Export Ltd
Zendegii Frill Limited
Zendegii Retail Limited
Zion Kitchen Limited
Zip & Zing Juices Ltd

Merseyside
Garden House Farms Limited
Restore Juice Co Ltd

Middlesex [11]
Afgdryfruites.co.uk Limited
Clynes Farms Ltd
Desert Raw Ltd
Green-Beam Life Limited
Perfect Brands (Europe) Ltd
Perfect Brands Ltd
Raw Candy Ltd
Rawness Limited
SVZ (UK) Limited
Tam Events & Cafe Ltd
Wellbeing and Balance Limited

Midlothian
Baxters Food Group Limited
Naturally Ugly Ltd
Pure Press Ltd
Seabuckthorn Scotland CIC

Monmouthshire
Kunubu Ltd

Norfolk
Dean Press Cider Ltd.
Andrew M Jarvis Limited
Sunrise Produce Ltd

Northamptonshire [5]
Alpro (UK) Limited
Coldpress Foods Limited
Glotedragon Ltd
Livewheatgrass Limited
Orchard House Foods Limited

Nottinghamshire [5]
Academic Fruits Limited
Drinks Group Holdings Ltd
Earthstrong Juicery Ltd
Spnet Ltd.
Vegan Monster Ltd

Oxfordshire [9]
CPRESS One Limited
Food Development Co Ltd
Nourish Juice Ltd
Oxford Juice Co Ltd
Rootyfruit Limited
Tiddly Pommes Ltd
Waterperry Gardens Limited
Wonky Food Limited
Wonky Group Ltd

Powys
Direct Ingredients Limited
Ingredients Direct (UK) Ltd

Somerset [5]
Bradleys Juices Limited
Ben Crossman Limited
Go Super You Limited
Simply Great Drinks (Europe) Ltd
F. A. Young Farm Produce Ltd

Staffordshire
Bimim Foods Limited
Felukka Limited

Suffolk
Fitness Fruits Limited
H & D Ventures Limited

Surrey [13]
Ariana Foods (PVT) Ltd
Brew Crew & Co. Limited
Chocquers Limited
Dr. Chocolate Limited
Eye Adom Market Limited
Fruiture Ltd
Grace Under Pressure Ltd
Healthy Thirst Drinks Limited
J.T Freshly Limited
Juice A Day Limited
Juice Smith Limited
Juicyology Ltd
Pressed Ltd

Sussex [5]
Cowdray Live Ltd.
Fruit International Limited
Juice 1st Limited
Natvitanet Ltd
Verjuice Limited

Tyne & Wear
Inside Armour Ltd
Juice Freaks Co Ltd

Warwickshire
Ultimate Juice Limited

West Midlands [9]
Bennu Rising Ltd.
Exclusively Unique Ltd
Fimivita Agrimining Limited

Juice Fit JQ Limited
Juice Garden Limited
Karrmancooks Ltd
Livitus Limited
Never Not Natural Ltd
Purer Ltd

Wiltshire
Handmade Cider Co Ltd
Juice Delivery Service Ltd
LB London Ltd

Worcestershire
Akiki Organics (UK) Limited

Yorkshire [8]
Bright Smoothies Ltd
Fruit and Veg Co Leeds Ltd
Get Fresh Ltd
Get Juiced (UK) Ltd
Hijama Ruqya Remedies Ltd
Impressive Juices Ltd
Sunlife Organics Limited
Truth Tonics Limited

Company Profiles

9 Pillars Ltd
Incorporated: 19 April 2018
Registered Office: The Old Barn, Wood Street, Swanley, Kent, BR8 7PA
Major Shareholder: Robert Nathaniel Cochrane
Officers: Robert Nathaniel Cochrane [1989] Director

A2A Foods Limited
Incorporated: 20 February 2016
Net Worth Deficit: £2,795
Registered Office: 16 Salisbury Court, Marlborough Drive, Basildon, Essex, SS16 6GA
Shareholders: Olrick Coker; Siobhan Coker
Officers: Olrick Coker [1985] Creative Director; Siobhan Coker [1985] Director/Maths Teacher

ABA Foods Limited
Incorporated: 19 November 2013
Net Worth: £26,307 *Total Assets:* £55,545
Registered Office: 25 Roxwell Trading Park, Argall Avenue, London, E10 7QY
Major Shareholder: Elizabeth Odame-Labi
Officers: Elizabeth Odame-Labi [1958] Director; Paula Odame-Labi [1991] Director/Teacher

Abanability Ltd
Incorporated: 22 August 2018
Registered Office: 63 Baptist Well Street, Swansea, SA1 6FB
Major Shareholder: Michael Powell
Officers: Michael Powell [1998] Director/Consultant

Academic Fruits Limited
Incorporated: 17 October 2018
Registered Office: 5 Belwood Close, Nottingham, NG11 8HZ
Major Shareholder: Miroslaw Marek Kasprzak
Officers: Dr. Miroslaw Marek Kasprzak [1984] Director [Polish]

Adunni Foods Ltd
Incorporated: 28 October 2011
Net Worth Deficit: £31,478 *Total Assets:* £956
Registered Office: 31 Glendale Avenue, Manchester, M19 1EH
Major Shareholder: Yetunde Folasade Bolarin
Officers: Yetunde Folasade Bolarin [1969] Director

Aero Cosmetics Limited
Incorporated: 6 July 2016
Registered Office: Apt 23552, Chynoweth House, Trevissome Park, Blackwater, Truro, Cornwall, TR4 8UN
Officers: Darren Hickling [1996] Director/Undergraduate

Affybale Ltd
Incorporated: 27 January 2016
Net Worth Deficit: £505
Registered Office: 9 Gaywood Close, London, SW2 3PN
Officers: Eno William Uffort, Secretary; Eno William Uffort [1973] Director/Musician; Affiong Uffort-Otuyelu [1974] Director/Store Manager

Afgdryfruites.co.uk Limited
Incorporated: 16 April 2018
Registered Office: 19 Stanwell Gardens, Staines upon Thames, Middlesex, TW19 7JY
Shareholder: Shafiqullah Taheri
Officers: Ahmad Mansoor Taheri [2001] Director [Afghan]

Agro Plus Limited
Incorporated: 5 June 2018
Registered Office: 9 Northbourne Way, Cliftonville, Margate, Kent, CT9 3NS
Officers: Damian Szymanski [1998] Director/Cook [Polish]

Akiki Organics (UK) Limited
Incorporated: 20 October 2016 *Employees:* 1
Net Worth Deficit: £2,932 *Total Assets:* £455
Registered Office: Thorneloe House, 25 Barbourne Road, Worcester, WR1 1RU
Major Shareholder: Charbel El-Akiki
Officers: Charbel El-Akiki [1968] Director

Alba of Tonbridge Limited
Incorporated: 10 July 2006
Net Worth: £5,130 *Total Assets:* £12,299
Registered Office: Three Counties House, 18a Victoria Street, Dunstable, Beds, LU6 3BA
Shareholder: Sarah Jane Parbery Faes
Officers: Nikolaas Francois Joanna Faes [1962] Director/Stockbroker [Belgian]; Sarah Jane Parbery Faes [1963] Director/Farmer

Alkalize Me Ltd
Incorporated: 21 November 2016
Net Worth: £21,708 *Total Assets:* £21,708
Registered Office: 4 Leegate, London, SE12 8SS
Major Shareholder: Phaik Khay Esther Chan
Officers: Esther Phaik Khay Chan [1973] Director/Senior Marketing Manager [Singaporean]; Wan-Hsuan Lin [1976] Director

Alpro (UK) Limited
Incorporated: 5 February 1999 *Employees:* 206
Net Worth: £48,926,000 *Total Assets:* £81,150,000
Registered Office: Latimer Business Park, Altendiez Way, Burton Latimer, Kettering, Northants, NN15 5YT
Parent: Alpro European Holdings S.A.R.L.
Officers: Paul Denayer, Secretary; Paul Denayer [1969] Finance & Administration Director [Belgian]; Sven Lamote [1973] Director [Belgian]; Yves Pellegrino [1965] Director/EVP Finance [French]

Amaze Offers Ltd
Incorporated: 22 January 2019
Registered Office: 68 Farnan Avenue, London, E17 4NG
Major Shareholder: Nikolay Blagoev Trenkov
Officers: Nikolay Blagoev Trenkov [1976] Director/Taxi Driver [Bulgarian]

AMC Freshly Squeezed (UK) Limited
Incorporated: 21 June 2018
Registered Office: Degrave House, Whitemoss Business Park, Skelmersdale, Lancs, WN8 9TQ
Parent: AMC Fresh Juices Investments (UK) Ltd
Officers: Deborah Frances Haigh, Secretary; Terence Richard James Haigh [1965] Director

AMM Ventures Ltd
Incorporated: 3 November 2015
Net Worth Deficit: £12,211 *Total Assets:* £237
Registered Office: 67 Delaware Mansions, Delaware Road, London, W9 2LJ
Major Shareholder: Denitsa Valerieva Gueorguieva
Officers: Denitsa Valerieva Gueorguieva [1985] Director [Bulgarian]

Ammo Your Ammunition to Greatness Limited
Incorporated: 7 October 2016
Registered Office: 4 Rochfords Gardens, Slough, Berks, SL2 5XJ
Officers: Sharmarke Haydar Ali [1993] Director

Analytical-Solutions UK Ltd
Incorporated: 20 March 2007
Net Worth: £14,452 *Total Assets:* £27,473
Registered Office: 106 Woodland Drive, St Albans, Herts, AL4 0ET
Major Shareholder: Yde Bouke Yntema
Officers: Anne Claire Bordier, Secretary; Yde Bouke Yntema [1969] Director/Analyst [Dutch]

Anglo African Food & Beverages Holding Ltd
Incorporated: 11 April 2018
Registered Office: 71-75 Shelton Street, London, WC2H 9JQ
Shareholders: Adebayo Adeosun; Carl Buddhasingh
Officers: Adebayo Adeosun [1966] Director; Carl Buddhasingh [1963] Director

Ariana Foods (PVT) Ltd
Incorporated: 9 September 2014
Registered Office: 115 London Road, Morden, Surrey, SM4 5HP
Shareholders: Hafeez Ullah; Asmatullah Khan
Officers: Liaqat Ali [1960] Director/Entrepreneur [Pakistani]; Asmatullah Khan [1978] Director/Entrepreneur [Pakistani]; Hafeez Ullah [1980] Director/Entrepreneur [Pakistani]

Armagh Juice Company Limited
Incorporated: 8 May 2017
Registered Office: 73 Drumnasoo Road, Portadown, Co Armagh, BT62 4EX
Officers: Kelly Crawford [1981] Director; Helen Troughton [1954] Director; Mark Troughton [1983] Director; Philip Troughton [1953] Director

Asher & Son (Fruit & Vegetable Supplies) Limited
Incorporated: 17 October 1979 *Employees:* 107
Net Worth: £1,442,482 *Total Assets:* £3,231,579
Registered Office: 1 Queens Parade, Brownlow Road, London, N11 2DN
Parent: Davin Foods Limited
Officers: Andriani Joannides, Secretary; Kyriacos Joannides [1969] Director/Company Manager

Aspire Better Health Limited
Incorporated: 18 February 2016
Registered Office: 117 Ellingham Way, Ashford, Kent, TN23 6LZ
Major Shareholder: Terje Sorken
Officers: Terje Sorken [1950] Director [Norwegian]

Avobravo Limited
Incorporated: 17 January 2017
Registered Office: 318 Norbury Avenue, London, SW16 3RL
Major Shareholder: Hamza Zaveri
Officers: Hamza Zaveri [1990] Director

AW Consultancy & Solutions Ltd
Incorporated: 16 January 2019
Registered Office: 130 Old Street, London, EC1V 9BD
Officers: Anthony Walsh [1971] Director

AWA Nature Ltd
Incorporated: 26 November 2018
Registered Office: 39 Park West, Kendal Street, London, W2 2QG
Major Shareholder: Houssein Awada
Officers: Houssein Awada, Secretary; Houssein Awada [1975] Director

Ayad Corporation Ltd
Incorporated: 5 July 2018
Registered Office: Tower 42, 25 Old Broad Street, London, EC2N 1HN
Officers: Youssri Ayadi [1995] Director/Founder [French]

Azalizo Foods Ltd
Incorporated: 13 April 2018
Registered Office: 55a Denmark Hill, London, SE5 8RS
Officers: Namulindwa Johansson [1989] Director [Swedish]

Bare Goodness Limited
Incorporated: 12 November 2018
Registered Office: 258a Norwood Road, London, SE27 9AJ
Major Shareholder: Paulette Thompson
Officers: Paulette Thompson [1960] Director [Canadian]

Barsupply Limited
Incorporated: 23 June 2016
Net Worth Deficit: £1,620 *Total Assets:* £23,902
Registered Office: JSA Partners Accountants, 41 Skylines Village, Isle of Dogs, London, E14 9TS
Shareholder: Vince Mate Toreki
Officers: Balazs Ferencz [1982] Director [Hungarian]; Vince Mate Toreki [1981] Director/IT Specialist [Hungarian]

Baxters Food Group Limited
Incorporated: 7 November 1945 *Employees:* 1,586
Net Worth: £78,064,000 *Total Assets:* £305,020,992
Registered Office: 12 Charlotte Square, Edinburgh, EH2 4DJ
Parent: W.A. Baxter & Sons (Holdings) Limited
Officers: Lucy Jill Strachan, Secretary; Audrey Caroline Baxter [1961] Director; Ronald Davis [1957] Director [American]; Michael Scott McGill [1968] Director

BB & F Consultants Limited
Incorporated: 1 September 2018
Registered Office: 20-22 Wenlock Road, London, N1 7GU
Major Shareholder: John James Fisher
Officers: John James Fisher [1971] Director/Consultant

Bear & Organics Limited
Incorporated: 25 May 2016
Registered Office: 7a Ridge Avenue, Marple, Stockport, Cheshire, SK6 7HJ
Major Shareholder: James Ainsley Wild
Officers: Sophie Alexandra Wild, Secretary; James Ainsley Wild [1988] Director/Founder

Bear Dough Limited
Incorporated: 30 April 2018
Registered Office: 43 Milkstone Road, Rochdale, Lancs, OL11 1EB
Officers: Tusif Khan [1984] Director

Beermats4u Limited
Incorporated: 19 March 2015
Net Worth: £25,855 *Total Assets:* £48,605
Registered Office: 16 Beaufort Court, Admirals Way, Docklands, London, E14 9XL
Shareholders: Lukinus Schoonhoven; Rajimi Schoomhoven
Officers: Rajimi Schoomhoven [1987] Director [Dutch]; Lukinus Schoonhoven [1954] Director/Manager [Dutch]

Benburb Bramleys Limited
Incorporated: 29 October 1981 *Employees:* 27
Net Worth: £1,487,495 *Total Assets:* £2,657,777
Registered Office: 228 Derryfubble Road, Benburb, Co Tyrone, BT71 7JS
Officers: Shirley Ann Willis, Secretary; Shirley Ann Willis [1961] Director; Thomas David Willis [1956] Director/Farmer

Bennu Rising Ltd.
Incorporated: 31 January 2019
Registered Office: Fort Dunlop, Fort Parkway, Birmingham, B24 9FE
Shareholders: Joseph Burris; Mizani Bennu
Officers: Joseph Burris [1988] Director/Entrepreneur

Bensons Fruit Juice Limited
Incorporated: 21 August 2002 *Employees:* 15
Net Worth: £128,992 *Total Assets:* £590,317
Registered Office: Sandyhill Farm, Sherborne, Glos, GL54 3DS
Shareholders: Alexia Louise Benson; Jeremy Benson
Officers: Alexia Benson, Secretary; Alexia Louise Benson [1973] Director; Jeremy Benson [1971] Director

Berrybegood Ltd
Incorporated: 13 February 2018
Registered Office: Semper Viridis, 23 Mills Chase, Bracknell, Berks, RG12 9RE
Officers: Silvia Thomas [1968] Director

Bimim Foods Limited
Incorporated: 22 December 2017
Registered Office: Bimim Foods Limited, 3711 Leek Road, Stoke on Trent, Staffs, ST4 9NN
Major Shareholder: Badrul Miah
Officers: Badrul Miah [1996] Managing Director

Borderless Catering Ltd
Incorporated: 12 June 2017
Registered Office: International House, 24 Holborn Viaduct, London, EC1A 2BN
Officers: Marie-Olive Akinrinlude [1996] Director

Bradleys Juices Limited
Incorporated: 23 July 2012 *Employees:* 7
Net Worth Deficit: £7,863 *Total Assets:* £283,747
Registered Office: Spencer House, 6 Morston Court, Aisecombe Way, Weston Super Mare, Somerset, BS22 8NA
Shareholders: Elizabeth Madeleine Bradley; John Miles Bradley; John Miles Bradley
Officers: Elizabeth Madeleine Bradley, Secretary; Elizabeth Madeleine Bradley [1960] Director; John Miles Bradley [1956] Director

Brew Crew & Co. Limited
Incorporated: 10 April 2017
Registered Office: 9 Windmill Terrace, Walton Bridge Road, Shepperton, Surrey, TW17 8ND
Shareholders: Patrick Jonathan Joseph Moorhead; Claire Elizabeth Moorhead
Officers: Patrick Jonathan Joseph Moorhead [1983] Managing Director [Irish]

Bright Smoothies Ltd
Incorporated: 21 February 2019
Registered Office: 49 Westfield Road, Leeds, LS3 1DF
Major Shareholder: Lewis Dan Challinor
Officers: Lewis Dan Challinor [1994] Director/Student

Bringing Eden Ltd
Incorporated: 7 February 2018
Registered Office: Soapbox, Old Street, London, EC1V 9HX
Major Shareholder: Osman Enver
Officers: Osman Enver [1993] Director/Support Worker

BSP Juice Ltd
Incorporated: 6 February 2018
Registered Office: 34 Croydon Road, London, E13 8ET
Major Shareholder: Dolly Parvin
Officers: Dolly Parvin, Secretary; Dolly Parvin [1980] Director

Cafe Tani Limited
Incorporated: 12 February 2018
Registered Office: 254 Seven Sisters Road, London, N4 2HY
Officers: Faisal Masoud [1982] Director/Cafe

Califia Farms UK Limited
Incorporated: 1 February 2017
Registered Office: c/o Grant Thornton Company Secretarial Services, 30 Finsbury Square, London, EC2A 1AG
Officers: Greg Steltenpohl [1954] Director [American]

California Girl Foods Ltd
Incorporated: 24 July 2012
Registered Office: 3 The Courtyard, Parsonage Farm, Throwley, Faversham, Kent, ME13 0ET
Major Shareholder: Carol Cunningham
Officers: Carol Cunningham [1956] Director/Physician [American]

The Cane Press Ltd
Incorporated: 12 March 2018
Registered Office: 20-22 Wenlock Road, London, N1 7GU
Major Shareholder: Dawn Wilson
Officers: Dawn Wilson [1984] Director

Carbon Fresh Limited
Incorporated: 10 February 2016
Registered Office: Number 14, 106 Southampton Row, London, WC1B 4BP
Shareholders: Kevin Helton; Jane Erica Hutchison
Officers: Kevin Helton [1979] Director/Designer; Jane Erica Hutchison [1976] Director/Designer

CCM Enterprises Limited
Incorporated: 27 November 2015
Net Worth Deficit: £38,554 *Total Assets:* £10,025
Registered Office: 20-22 Wenlock Road, London, N1 7GU
Shareholders: Eduardo Jose Clavijo; Kevin Meehan
Officers: Kevin Meehan, Secretary; Eduardo Jose Clavijo [1972] Director [Spanish]; Kevin Andrew Meehan [1966] Director

Chakra Chai Limited
Incorporated: 6 March 2018
Registered Office: 39 Kingsmill Terrace, London, NW8 6AA
Major Shareholder: Hoda Mohajerani
Officers: Hoda Mohajerani [1971] Founder & Director

Chakra Shots Limited
Incorporated: 27 February 2019
Registered Office: Flat 13, Agricola Court, 82 Parnell Road, London, E3 2RY
Officers: Regina Ward, Secretary; Regina Ann Elizabeth Ward [1966] Director [Irish]

Chefs Food Products Ltd
Incorporated: 16 July 2018
Registered Office: 71-75 Shelton Street, London, WC2H 9JQ
Major Shareholder: Mohammad Amash Duraiz
Officers: Mohammad Amash Duraiz [1991] Director

Chiltern Ridge Apple Juice Limited
Incorporated: 24 August 2011
Net Worth: £7,044 *Total Assets:* £63,194
Registered Office: Brandon House, 90 The Broadway, Chesham, Bucks, HP5 1EG
Shareholders: Evert Donker; Franca Sonja Den Breejen Van Den Bout
Officers: Evert Donker [1961] Director/Manager [Dutch]

Chocquers Limited
Incorporated: 5 March 2015
Registered Office: 49 Upper Selsdon Road, South Croydon, Surrey, CR2 8DG
Officers: Paul Abdul-Abbass Audu [1966] Director/Consultant; Sharon Johnson [1962] Director/Consultant

Claense Ltd
Incorporated: 31 August 2017
Registered Office: 19b Rucklidge Avenue, London, NW10 4QA
Officers: John Anthony Pinto Morais [1991] Director/Exercise Specialist

Clearly Juice Limited
Incorporated: 26 April 2012
Registered Office: 5th Floor, Ashford Commercial Quarter, 1 Dover Place, Ashford, Kent, TN23 1FB
Shareholders: Richard Julian Barnes; Sally Barnes
Officers: Richard Julian Barnes [1960] Director; Sally Barnes [1961] Director

Clynes Farms Ltd
Incorporated: 25 May 2017
Registered Office: 11 Clynes House, Attlee Road, Hayes, Middlesex, UB4 9JA
Officers: Eke Ijuo [1979] Director/Farmer [Nigerian]; Joseph Ijuo Ikpe-Adegwu [1970] Director/Farmer

Coco Twist Ltd
Incorporated: 10 March 2018
Registered Office: 16 Leicester Road, Blaby, Leicester, LE8 4GQ
Major Shareholder: Akash Deep Singh Kular
Officers: Akash Deep Singh Kular [1976] Managing Director

Coldpress Foods Limited
Incorporated: 5 July 2011 *Employees:* 9
Net Worth: £476,422 *Total Assets:* £1,861,154
Registered Office: 1 Rushmills, Northampton, NN4 7YB
Shareholder: Chloe Gibb
Officers: Andrew Donald Bruce Gibb [1966] Director/Business Marketing Consultant [Australian]; Chloe Samantha Gibb [1972] Director/Life Coach [Australian]

Coton Orchard Limited
Incorporated: 27 December 1995 *Employees:* 4
Net Worth: £613,526 *Total Assets:* £681,787
Registered Office: Landbeach Lakes, Ely Road, Waterbeach, Cambridge, CB25 9PG
Officers: Michael George Lenoir, Secretary; Albert Edward Gazeley [1937] Director; Anna Teresa Gazeley [1970] Director/Accountant; Supanee Gazeley [1939] Director

The Cotswold Fruit Company Ltd.
Incorporated: 20 November 2014
Net Worth Deficit: £49,867 *Total Assets:* £17,607
Registered Office: Bleby House, Abbey Terrace, Winchcombe, Cheltenham, Glos, GL54 5LL
Major Shareholder: David Richard Lindgren
Officers: Frances Bryony House [1966] Director; David Richard Lindgren [1961] Business Development Director

Cowdray Live Ltd.
Incorporated: 10 February 2014
Net Worth Deficit: £15,223
Registered Office: Cowdray Estate Office, Easebourne, Midhurst, W Sussex, GU29 0AQ
Major Shareholder: Honourable Emily Pearson
Officers: Honourable Emily Pearson [1989] Director/Raw Food Juice Bar

Cowherds Juicery Limited
Incorporated: 23 March 2018
Registered Office: 28 Squires Lane, Tyldesley, Manchester, M29 8JF
Shareholders: Paula Michelle Maguire; Jon Shepherd-Smyth
Officers: Paula Michelle Maguire [1980] Director; Jon Shepherd-Smyth [1985] Director

CPJLondon Ltd
Incorporated: 12 December 2016
Net Worth: £1 *Total Assets:* £780,051
Registered Office: 243 St Albans Road, Watford, Herts, WD24 5BQ
Officers: Mark Cook [1963] Director; Haseeb Ghuman [1993] Sales Director

CPRESS One Limited
Incorporated: 23 April 2014 *Employees:* 8
Net Worth Deficit: £558,652 *Total Assets:* £314,298
Registered Office: 6a St Andrews Court, Wellington Street, Thame, Oxon, OX9 3WT
Parent: CPRESS Management Limited
Officers: Timothy Vernon King Stevenson [1981] Director/Private Equity [French]

Crosby Beverages Ltd
Incorporated: 19 February 2018
Registered Office: 193 Drayton Bridge Road, London, W13 0JH
Major Shareholder: Odi Olali
Officers: Rhys Johnson [1991] Director; Odi Olali [1990] Director

Ben Crossman Limited
Incorporated: 21 October 2005
Net Worth: £31,383 *Total Assets:* £87,091
Registered Office: Mayfield Farm, Hewish, Weston-Super-Mare, Somerset, BS24 6RQ
Major Shareholder: Benjamin Crossman
Officers: Benjamin Andrew Crossman [1955] Director/Farmer and Cider Maker

Crown of Life Juices Ltd
Incorporated: 9 October 2013
Net Worth Deficit: £37,068 *Total Assets:* £661
Registered Office: 16 Herbert Road, Ramsgate, Kent, CT11 0AS
Major Shareholder: Stephen James Court
Officers: Stephen James Court [1975] Director/Property Landlord

J.C.Davies & Hall Limited
Incorporated: 10 January 2017
Net Worth Deficit: £136 *Total Assets:* £250
Registered Office: The Townsend Farm, Stretton Grandison, Ledbury, Herefords, HR8 2TS
Officers: Malcolm Davies [1955] Director/Farmer; James Hall [1987] Director/Wholesale

Dboost Drinks Limited
Incorporated: 4 April 2018
Registered Office: Bate Mill Farmhouse, Batemill Lane, Chelford, Macclesfield, Cheshire, SK11 9BW
Shareholders: Robert Dry; Sharon Dry
Officers: Robert Dry [1966] Marketing Director; Sharon Dry [1968] Director/Marketing Manager

Dean Press Cider Ltd.
Incorporated: 17 October 2017
Registered Office: Underdean House, Newnham Road, Blakeney, Norfolk, GL15 4AE
Major Shareholder: Christopher Michael Peter Fordham
Officers: Christopher Michael Peter Fordham [1983] Director

Degarnix Ltd
Incorporated: 11 September 2017
Registered Office: 73 Cosmeston Street, Cardiff, CF24 4LQ
Major Shareholder: Daisy Udeze
Officers: Daisy Udeze [1967] Director

Demcar UK Limited
Incorporated: 2 March 2015
Net Worth: £8,973 *Total Assets:* £10,348
Registered Office: 1st Floor, 2 Woodberry Grove, Finchley, London, N12 0DR
Shareholders: Simone Beckles; Colin Beckles
Officers: Mark-Anthony Trevon Beckles, Secretary; Colin Beckles [1960] Director/Businessman [Guyanese]; Simone Beckles [1970] Director/Nurse [Guyanese]

Desert Raw Ltd
Incorporated: 8 March 2018
Registered Office: 102 Victor Road, Middlesex, Teddington, Middlesex, TW11 3AS
Officers: Sophie Ann Middleton, Secretary; Phoebe Middleton [1986] Director/Designer

Devon Garden Foods Limited
Incorporated: 19 January 2018
Registered Office: Exeter Science Park, 6 Babbage Way, Clyst, Honiton, Exeter, EX5 2FN
Major Shareholder: Cesar Enrique Torres Ledezma
Officers: Cesar Enrique Torres Ledezma [1977] Director/Founder

Devon Orchard Ltd
Incorporated: 12 March 2014
Net Worth Deficit: £4,676 *Total Assets:* £3,503
Registered Office: 50 Cowick Street, Exeter, EX4 1AP
Officers: Caroline Wilson [1956] Director/Senior Community Carer; Martin Geoffrey Wilson [1953] Director/Estimator

Direct Ingredients Limited
Incorporated: 15 February 2005
Registered Office: Unit 2 Warren Road, Brecon Enterprise Park, Brecon, Powys, LD3 8BT
Officers: Edward Thomas Gough, Secretary/Director; Edward Thomas Gough [1973] Director; Raemonde Jones [1946] Director

The Dirty Milkshake Ltd
Incorporated: 28 November 2018
Registered Office: 71 Adriatic Apartments, 20 Western Gateway, London, E16 1BT
Major Shareholder: Claudia Covatariu
Officers: Claudia Covatariu [1991] Director/General Manager [Romanian]; MD Yasin Dewan [1989] Director/Customer Care [Bangladeshi]

Dnajuices Limited
Incorporated: 16 August 2017
Registered Office: Unit 4, 345 North End Road, London, SW6 1NN
Major Shareholder: Matthew Patrick Burns
Officers: Matthew Patrick Burns [1992] Managing Director

TJ & PJ Dobson Ltd
Incorporated: 21 February 2006
Net Worth Deficit: £305,436 *Total Assets:* £342,145
Registered Office: 255 Hartford Road, Davenham, Northwich, Cheshire, CW9 8JT
Major Shareholder: Thomas Jonathan Dobson
Officers: Philip John Dobson, Secretary; Jean Mary Dobson [1954] Director/Teacher; Philip John Dobson [1951] Director/Builder; Thomas Jonathan Dobson [1982] Director/Fire Fighter

Doromomo & Sons Ltd
Incorporated: 8 May 2018
Registered Office: 198 High Street, Tonbridge, Kent, TN9 1BE
Shareholders: Winston Rainer Cuthbert; Aidan Julius Lethem
Officers: Aidan Julius Lethem [1994] Director

Dr. Chocolate Limited
Incorporated: 14 August 2018
Registered Office: 18 Church Rise, Chessington, Surrey, KT9 2EZ
Officers: Jacqueline Caws [1966] Director

The Drinks Group Holdings Ltd
Incorporated: 3 October 2018
Registered Office: Mercury House, Shipstones Business Centre, Northgate, Nottingham, NG7 7FN
Major Shareholder: Peter Robson
Officers: Peter Robson, Secretary; Peter Robson [1959] Director

DrJuicy Ltd
Incorporated: 4 April 2018
Registered Office: 9 Ivatt Place, West Kensington, London, W14 9NQ
Shareholders: Lancelot Clive Webb; Junior Webb
Officers: Andre Grant, Secretary; Junior Webb, Secretary; Junior Webb [1987] Director/Operations Manager; Lancelot Clive Webb [1957] Director/Juice Maker

Duskin Farm Limited
Incorporated: 1 May 1964 *Employees:* 5
Net Worth: £1,562,669 *Total Assets:* £2,032,433
Registered Office: Duskin Farm, Kingston, Canterbury, Kent, CT4 6JS
Shareholders: Pamela Jean Helbling; Andrew Alistair Helbling
Officers: Andrew Alistair Helbling [1939] Director; Susan Jane Helbling [1974] Director/General Manager

Dzatafia Ltd
Incorporated: 18 December 2018
Registered Office: Kemp House, 160 City Road, London, EC1V 2NX
Major Shareholder: Benjamin Adzofu
Officers: Benjamin Adzofu, Secretary; Benjamin Adzofu [1974] Director

Earthstrong Juicery Ltd
Incorporated: 3 October 2018
Registered Office: 9 Lees Hill Street, Nottingham, NG2 4JW
Major Shareholder: Jordan Blake Summers
Officers: Jordan Blake Summers [1993] Director/Quality Assurance Analyst

Elgin's Orchard Ltd
Incorporated: 21 August 2017 *Employees:* 3
Net Worth Deficit: £23,778 *Total Assets:* £71,662
Registered Office: Kirkhill House, Elgin, Moray, IV30 5NZ
Shareholders: Roy Matheson; Valerie Elizabeth Matheson
Officers: Angus Martin Dixon [1963] Director/Forester; Roy Matheson [1945] Director/Farmer; Valerie Elizabeth Matheson [1939] Director/Farmer

Ella Drinks Limited
Incorporated: 20 October 1998
Net Worth: £103,308 *Total Assets:* £470,776
Registered Office: Wandershiell, Aldbar, Brechin, Angus, DD9 6SY
Shareholders: Anne Thomson; John Stephen Gallagher
Officers: Anne Thomson, Secretary; John Stephen Gallagher [1952] Director; Anne Thomson [1954] Director

Elmsfield Enterprises Limited
Incorporated: 1 September 2004
Registered Office: 8 Falconwood Parade, Welling, Kent, DA16 2PL
Shareholder: The International Law Firm Ltd
Officers: Muhammad Muneer [1959] Managing Director [Bangladeshi]; Christopher Geden Wallis [1949] Director/Manager

Endurance Juice Company Limited
Incorporated: 14 April 2009
Registered Office: 6 Pulford Road, London, N15 6SP
Major Shareholder: Michael Osizimhete Okpapi
Officers: John Ikhaobomhe Okpapi, Secretary; John Ikhaobomhe Okpapi [1989] Director/Company Secretary & Deputy Chief Executive Officer; Michael Osizimhete Okpapi [1959] Director/Chairman & Chief Executive Officer

Ethically Made Ltd
Incorporated: 15 October 2018
Registered Office: 50 Cambridge Road, Barking, Essex, IG11 8FG
Major Shareholder: Giuseppe Baidoo
Officers: Giuseppe Baidoo [1990] Director [Italian]

Exclusively Unique Ltd
Incorporated: 19 June 2018
Registered Office: 71 Tempest Steet, Wolverhampton, W Midlands, WV2 1AA
Major Shareholder: Daliah Browne
Officers: Tiyanna Browne, Secretary; Daliah Browne [1970] Director/Cosmetologist

Eye Adom Market Limited
Incorporated: 20 June 2017
Registered Office: 39 Brigstock Road, Thornton Heath, Croydon, Surrey, CR7 7JH
Officers: Joseph Danquah [1974] Director/Retailer [Italian]; Henrietta Opoku [1959] Director

Felukka Limited
Incorporated: 24 February 2010
Registered Office: Cannock Chase Enterprise Centre, Hednesford, Cannock, Staffs, WS12 0QU
Officers: Charles Bond Foster [1955] Director

Fimivita Agrimining Limited
Incorporated: 10 June 2016
Net Worth Deficit: £72
Registered Office: Flat 46, Bromford Drive, Hodge Hill, Birmingham, B36 8RB
Officers: Alfred Musasa Manziala [1958] Director/Researcher

Fitness Fruits Limited
Incorporated: 30 November 2017
Registered Office: Cardinal House, 46 St Nicholas Street, Ipswich, Suffolk, IP1 1TT
Major Shareholder: Jordan Barrow
Officers: Jordan Barrow, Secretary; Jordan Barrow [1991] Managing Director

The Food and Drink Development Company Limited
Incorporated: 19 December 2017
Registered Office: 12 Dewe Lane, Burghfield, Reading, Berks, RG30 3SU
Major Shareholder: Ketan Harshad Joshi
Officers: Carolynne Joshi, Secretary; Dev Ketan Kong Joshi [1994] Director; Jay Ketan Kong Joshi [1992] Director; Dr Ketan Harshad Joshi [1961] Director

Food Development Company Limited
Incorporated: 7 September 2009
Net Worth: £317,936 *Total Assets:* £416,502
Registered Office: 32 Oakley Road, Chinnor, Oxon, OX39 4HB
Officers: Sir Norman Murray Pringle, Secretary; Sir Norman Murray Pringle [1941] Director/Chartered Management Accountant; James Wilson Turnbull [1951] Director/Management Consultant

Four Elms Fruit Farm Limited
Incorporated: 16 May 2002
Net Worth: £161 *Total Assets:* £401,940
Registered Office: Woodlands, Harpford, Sidmouth, Devon, EX10 0NJ
Shareholder: Richard John Smedley
Officers: Pamela Ann Smedley [1931] Director; Richard John Smedley [1959] Director; Susan Jane Smedley [1962] Director

Four Elms Juice Limited
Incorporated: 2 June 2014
Net Worth: £158,557 *Total Assets:* £180,193
Registered Office: Four Elms Fruit Farm, Harpford, Sidmouth, Devon, EX10 0NJ
Shareholders: Richard John Smedley; Susan Jane Smedley
Officers: Richard John Smedley [1959] Director; Susan Jane Smedley [1962] Director

Fresh Appeal Limited
Incorporated: 23 June 2009
Registered Office: Fleet Estate Office, Manor Farm, Holbeach Hurn, Spalding, Lincs, PE12 8LR
Officers: Mark Richard Henson, Secretary; Martin John Taylor [1971] Group Managing Director; Duncan Richard Worth [1965] Director

Fresh Bagels Ltd.
Incorporated: 3 November 2017
Registered Office: 85 Biscay Road, London, W6 8JW
Major Shareholder: Emerson Hill
Officers: Emerson Hill [1991] Corporate Director

Fresh Manchester Ltd
Incorporated: 28 February 2019
Registered Office: 22 Fontwell Close, Manchester, M16 9RN
Major Shareholder: Kevin Paul Barry
Officers: Kevin Paul Barry [1970] Director/Juice Maker [Irish]

Fresh Trading Limited
Incorporated: 25 February 1999
Net Worth: £32,088,000 *Total Assets:* £49,264,000
Registered Office: 342 Ladbroke Grove, London, W10 5BU
Parent: European Refreshments
Officers: James Lewis Davenport, Secretary; James Lewis Davenport [1973] Director; Douglas Ross Lamont [1973] Director; Scott Edward Roche [1964] Director [Canadian]

Freshleigh Ltd
Incorporated: 11 February 2019
Registered Office: 2 Nelson Road, Leigh on Sea, Essex, SS9 3HU
Major Shareholder: Dannielle Lauren Emery
Officers: Dannielle Lauren Emery [1988] Director

Frol Explorer Ltd
Incorporated: 14 June 2018
Registered Office: Flat 5000, Kemp House, City Road, London, EC1V 2NX
Major Shareholder: Pedro Miguel Pereira Rodrigues
Officers: Manuel Carlos Seara Costa [1969] Director [Portuguese]

The Frozen Cocktail Company Limited
Incorporated: 16 August 2010
Registered Office: Office F, Consett Business Park, Villa Real, Consett, Co Durham, DH8 6BP
Shareholders: Lee Scott Hillary; Philip Rowland
Officers: Lee Scott Hillary [1972] Director; Phillip Rowland [1953] Director/Accountant

Frozenbeep Ltd
Incorporated: 11 July 2018
Registered Office: Suite 6, First Floor, Wordsworth Mill, Wordsworth Street, Bolton, Lancs, BL1 3ND
Major Shareholder: Benjamin Townsend
Officers: Ailyn Tiglao [1977] Director [Filipino]

Frugo Smoothies Ltd
Incorporated: 1 September 2016
Net Worth: £2,817 *Total Assets:* £13,136
Registered Office: 55 Stanworth Avenue, Bolton, Lancs, BL2 6EW
Shareholder: Michal Soroka
Officers: Ewa Soroka, Secretary; Ewa Stanislawa Soroka [1982] Director/Bar Manager [Polish]; Michal Soroka [1985] Director/Bar Manager [Polish]

The Fruit and Veg Co Leeds Ltd
Incorporated: 14 May 2018
Registered Office: 3 Whinmoor Mews, Leeds, LS14 5BX
Major Shareholder: James Dean Hawkins
Officers: James Dean Hawkins [1993] Director

Fruit International Limited
Incorporated: 31 August 2018
Registered Office: 11 Barker Close, Fishbourne, Chichester, W Sussex, PO18 8BJ
Major Shareholder: Monica Frances Jervis
Officers: Monica Frances Jervis [1963] Director/Accountant

Fruit Smoothies Ltd
Incorporated: 15 May 2009
Registered Office: 255 Hartford Road, Davenham, Northwich, Cheshire, CW9 8JT
Major Shareholder: Thomas Jonathan Dobson
Officers: Thomas Jonathan Dobson [1982] Director

Fruitapeel (Juice) Ltd
Incorporated: 11 September 2014 *Employees:* 89
Net Worth Deficit: £4,486,452 *Total Assets:* £11,136,089
Registered Office: Unit 2 Llantrisant Business Park, Llantrisant, Pontyclun, Mid Glamorgan, CF72 8LF
Shareholders: William Howard Porter; Terence Richard James Haigh
Officers: Andrew James Rooke [1971] Finance Director

Fruitful Durham Community Interest Company
Incorporated: 5 July 2012
Net Worth Deficit: £14 *Total Assets:* £3,143
Registered Office: 33 Arthur Street, Ushaw Moor, Co Durham, DH7 7PF
Officers: James Alaric Colville [1985] Director/Coach Driver; Julian Ashley Godfrey [1973] Director/Gardener; Rachel May Kurtz [1970] Director/Teacher; Janet Mary Tayler [1954] Director/Teacher

Fruitfullest Ltd.
Incorporated: 22 January 2019
Registered Office: 27 Hartington Road, Walthamstow, London, E17 8AS
Major Shareholder: Mohamed Saber Khemdoudi
Officers: Mohamed Saber Khemdoudi [1989] Director/Security Guard

FruitFullFruits Ltd
Incorporated: 24 October 2018
Registered Office: 130 Old Street, London, EC1V 9BD
Officers: Emma Ajose, Secretary; Emmanuel Ajose [1985] Director; Renell Hope Web [1988] Director/HGV Driver

Fruiture Ltd
Incorporated: 25 January 2019
Registered Office: 8 Warham Road, South Croydon, Surrey, CR2 6LE
Major Shareholder: Simone Shushannah Irving
Officers: Simone Shushannah Irving [1986] Director/General Manager

Funtime Products Limited
Incorporated: 24 November 2015
Registered Office: Flat 17, Oak House, 159 Croydon Road, London, SE20 7UB
Major Shareholder: Dunstan Godfrey Holder
Officers: Dunstan Godfrey Holder [1951] Managing Director; Yvette Anne Holder [1948] Director

Garden House Farms Limited
Incorporated: 6 October 2004
Net Worth: £21,236 *Total Assets:* £54,340
Registered Office: 7 Roe Lane, Southport, Merseyside, PR9 9DT
Major Shareholder: Anthony Thomas Harrison
Officers: Lord Antony Thomas Harrison [1961] Director

Garden Press Ltd
Incorporated: 5 July 2016
Net Worth Deficit: £14,652 *Total Assets:* £23,381
Registered Office: 49 Atlantic Business Centre, Atlantic Street, Broadheath, Altrincham, Cheshire, WA14 5NQ
Officers: Stephen Donovan [1961] Director; Chris Mosley [1985] Director/Account Manager; Kate Frances Mosley [1987] Director; Amy Victoria Shepherdson [1986] Director

Gerries Fruit Limited
Incorporated: 13 October 2010
Net Worth: £1,743 *Total Assets:* £1,742
Registered Office: Maple House, High Street, Potters Bar, Herts, EN6 5BS
Officers: Johannes Frederik Karel Nooteboom, Secretary; Gerritje Van Der Snel-Nooteboom [1941] Director [Dutch]

Get Fresh Ltd
Incorporated: 30 April 2018
Registered Office: 23-25 Cross Square, Wakefield, W Yorks, WF1 1PQ
Officers: Abdul Naeem [1971] Director/Electrical Engineer [Afghan]

Get Juiced (UK) Ltd
Incorporated: 23 September 2014
Net Worth Deficit: £99,486 *Total Assets:* £4,809
Registered Office: Wembley Works, Hemingfield Road, Wombwell, Barnsley, S Yorks, S73 0LY
Officers: Abaidullah Qasim [1985] Director [Pakistani]

Get Juiced Tooting Ltd
Incorporated: 31 January 2019
Registered Office: Get Juiced, Unit 15 Tooting Market, Tooting Broadway, Wandsworth, London, SW17 0SN
Major Shareholder: Leon David Anthony Morant
Officers: Leon David Morant [1987] Director/Manager

Gilt & Flint Ltd
Incorporated: 19 September 2018
Registered Office: Haye Farm, Musbury, Axminster, Devon, EX13 8ST
Shareholders: Daniel Paul Fitzpatrick; Harry Luca Boglione; Jason Samuel Slade
Officers: Harry Luca Boglione [1990] Director [Australian/Italian]; Daniel Paul Fitzpatrick [1974] Director; Jason Samuel Slade [1972] Director

Glotedragon Ltd
Incorporated: 22 July 2018
Registered Office: 214a Kettering Road, Northampton, NN1 4BN
Shareholders: Vita Bustillo; Jordan Hibbert
Officers: Vita Bustillo [1970] Director [Filipino]

Go Fresh Ltd
Incorporated: 14 December 2017
Registered Office: 20-22 Wenlock Road, London, N1 7GU
Major Shareholder: Jesvinder Devi
Officers: Jesvinder Devi [1970] Director/Project Manager

Go Super You Limited
Incorporated: 10 January 2018
Registered Office: 141 Englishcombe Lane, Bath, BA2 2EL
Shareholders: Lara Clifford; Henry Carpenter
Officers: Henry Carpenter [1977] Director; Lara Clifford [1977] Director

Gold Star Soft Drinks Westcountry Limited
Incorporated: 18 December 2009
Net Worth: £6,977 *Total Assets:* £129,558
Registered Office: 15 Bradfield Close, Leigham, Plymouth, PL6 8NG
Major Shareholder: Roger Melville Jolly
Officers: Roger Melville Jolly [1959] Director/Manager

Golden Hibiscus Foods and Drinks Ltd
Incorporated: 23 January 2018
Registered Office: Kemp House, 160 City Road, London, EC1V 2NX
Major Shareholder: Adeyemi Aiyewumi
Officers: Adeyemi Aiyewumi [1980] Director/Project Manager; Steven Aiyewumi [1976] Director/Project Manager

The Good Juice Company Limited
Incorporated: 11 December 2018
Registered Office: 7 Willow Road, Dunmow, Essex, CM6 1WD
Major Shareholder: Kelly Oakes
Officers: Kelly Oakes [1980] Director/Marketing Consultant

The Good MLK Ltd
Incorporated: 24 July 2018
Registered Office: 39 Long Acre, London, WC2E 9LG
Major Shareholder: Lulwa Abdulrahman
Officers: Lulwa Abdulrahman [1989] Director [Saudi Arabian]

Good Natured (Happy Monkey) Ltd
Incorporated: 5 April 2007 *Employees:* 6
Previous: Good Natured Ltd.
Net Worth: £512,512 *Total Assets:* £1,221,809
Registered Office: Rushley Green Barn, Rosemary Lane, Castle Hedingham, Halstead, Essex, CO9 3AH
Shareholders: Gregory Thomas Boyle; Multiple Marketing Ltd
Officers: Judith Anne Gray, Secretary; Gregory Thomas Boyle [1964] Director

Grace Under Pressure Ltd
Incorporated: 17 July 2014
Net Worth Deficit: £535,029 *Total Assets:* £89,890
Registered Office: Unit 12 Trade City, Avro Way, Brooklands Business Park, Weybridge, Surrey, KT13 0YF
Shareholders: Jamie Moulding; Jessica Mary Moulding
Officers: Jamie Moulding [1974] Director; Jessica Mary Moulding [1986] Director

Green-Beam Life Limited
Incorporated: 21 April 2015
Registered Office: 15 Cochrane House, Cowley Road, Uxbridge, Middlesex, UB8 2DA
Officers: Ali Hussain Shah [1985] Director/Self Employed; Zayd Hussain Shah [1988] Director

Greenie's Smoothies Limited
Incorporated: 13 January 2017
Net Worth Deficit: £48,716
Registered Office: 60 Felbrigge Road, Ilford, Essex, IG3 8DP
Major Shareholder: Olayinka Ayodele Otokiti
Officers: Olayinka Ayodele Otokiti [1956] Director/Beauty Consultant

H & D Ventures Limited
Incorporated: 21 March 2017
Net Worth Deficit: £44,797 *Total Assets:* £24,557
Registered Office: The Old Rectory, Aspall, Stowmarket, Suffolk, IP14 6NY
Shareholders: Henry Chevallier Guild; David John Steward
Officers: Henry Chevallier Guild [1968] Director; David John Steward [1962] Director

H & R Partners Limited
Incorporated: 26 January 2016
Net Worth: £182,210 *Total Assets:* £196,745
Registered Office: Studio 2.08, Chester House, 1-2 Brixton Road, London, SW9 6DE
Shareholder: Yifei Deng
Officers: Abdihaking Hashi [1985] Director; Yusuf Ekow Obi Richardson [1984] Director

H2T Food & Drink Limited
Incorporated: 25 January 2019
Registered Office: c/o Lux-TSI Limited, Unit 1b Pencoed Technology Park, Pencoed, Bridgend, CF35 5AQ
Shareholders: First Brands International Limited; Twisted Orange Limited
Officers: Michael John Evans [1963] Director/Business Owner; Dr Louise Beverley Neilson [1969] Director/Business Owner

Hainan Super Industrial Limited
Incorporated: 17 January 2018
Registered Office: 10 Kiln Court, 18 Newell Street, London, E14 7JP
Major Shareholder: Jiang Peng
Officers: Jiang Peng [1974] Director

Handmade Cider Company Limited
Incorporated: 4 May 2010 *Employees:* 1
Net Worth Deficit: £4,601 *Total Assets:* £40,447
Registered Office: The Old Cider Shed, Slaughterford Mill, Slaughterford, Chippenham, Wilts, SN14 8RJ
Major Shareholder: Denis France
Officers: Denis France [1967] Director

Health Hut NW Ltd
Incorporated: 30 August 2018
Registered Office: 10a Market Street, Wigan, Lancs, WN1 1JN
Shareholders: Benjamin Moore; Darren Maxfield
Officers: Darren Maxfield [1987] Director; Benjamin Moore [1985] Director

Healthy Drinks & Smoothie Ltd
Incorporated: 7 February 2018
Registered Office: 18 Westonbirt Close, St Mellons, Cardiff, CF3 0JJ
Major Shareholder: Isatou Sinera
Officers: Isatou Sinera [1985] Director/General Manager

Healthy Thirst Drinks Limited
Incorporated: 1 October 1991
Net Worth Deficit: £83,280 *Total Assets:* £8,966
Registered Office: Thornycroft Farm, Thorncroft Drive, Leatherhead, Surrey, KT22 8JD
Shareholders: Frank Christoffel Van Ooijen; Jules Van Harn; Guy Woodall; Sheila Catherine Woodall
Officers: Frank Christoffel Van Ooijen, Secretary; Jules Van Harn [1975] Director [Dutch]; Frank Christoffel Van Ooijen [1965] Director/MD [Dutch]; Dr Guy Woodall [1954] Director; Sheila Catherine Woodall [1955] Director

Hero Solutions Limited
Incorporated: 4 October 2016
Net Worth: £19 *Total Assets:* £1,328
Registered Office: Flat 2, 382 Kingston Road, London, SW20 8LN
Major Shareholder: Andrew Donald McCarter
Officers: Andrew Donald McCarter [1981] Director/Business Analyst [South African]

Hibitala UK Limited
Incorporated: 12 April 2018
Registered Office: Bioenergy and Brewing Sciences Building, College Road, Sutton Bonington, Loughborough, Leics, LE12 5RD
Major Shareholder: Richard Stuart Worrall
Officers: Richard Stuart Worrall [1958] Director

Hidden Orchard Ltd
Incorporated: 30 January 2019
Registered Office: Unit 1a Herniss Business Park, Longdowns, Cornwall, TR10 9BZ
Major Shareholder: Jeffrey Charles Richard Bradley
Officers: Jeffrey Charles Richard Bradley, Secretary; Jeffrey Charles Richard Bradley [1976] Director/Drinks Producer

Hijama Ruqya Remedies Ltd
Incorporated: 8 December 2015
Registered Office: 29 Duckworth Grove, Bradford, W Yorks, BD9 5HQ
Officers: Mohammed Saleem Yasin [1977] Director/Natural Medicine

J.P Hinds Limited
Incorporated: 27 April 2017
Registered Office: 19 The Chase, London, SW16 3AE
Major Shareholder: Jordan Patrick, Hakim Hinds
Officers: Jordan Patrick Hinds [1997] Director/Food and Drink

The Holy Grain Company Ltd.
Incorporated: 27 July 2015
Net Worth: £904 *Total Assets:* £904
Registered Office: 15 Sheldon Close, Lee, London, SE12 8UP
Major Shareholder: Jourdan Copeland
Officers: Jourdan Copeland [1993] Director/Model

Honestly Limited
Incorporated: 14 November 2017
Registered Office: 1 Scotswood Walk, Northumberland Park, Tottenham, London, N17 0TF
Major Shareholder: Chika Nnadozie Osamwonyi Ezenekwe Jr
Officers: Chika Nnadozie Osamwonyi Ezenekwe Jr [1997] Director Chief Executive

Hunterworth Ltd
Incorporated: 2 February 2017
Registered Office: 18 Cloudesley Place, Islington, London, N1 0JA
Major Shareholder: Laide Odeniyi
Officers: Laide Odeniyi [1968] Director/IT

Ice N Creamz Limited
Incorporated: 1 November 2017
Registered Office: 276 Markhouse Road, London, E17 8EF
Major Shareholder: Amani Campbell
Officers: Amani Campbell [1989] Director/Business Owner

Impressive Juices Ltd
Incorporated: 22 May 2015
Net Worth: £262 *Total Assets:* £262
Registered Office: Briar Rose, Silver Street, Whitley, Goole, E Yorks, DN14 0JG
Officers: Sarah Mary Helen Dowson [1969] Director/Teaching Assistant; Paula Melinda Murgatroyd [1970] Director/Administrative Assistant

Ingredients Direct (UK) Limited
Incorporated: 15 February 2005
Registered Office: Unit 2 Warren Road, Brecon Enterprise Park, Brecon, Powys, LD3 8BT
Officers: Edward Thomas Gough, Secretary/Director; Edward Thomas Gough [1973] Director; Raemonde Jones [1946] Director

Innocent Limited
Incorporated: 2 June 2000 *Employees:* 295
Net Worth: £49,300,000 *Total Assets:* £121,799,000
Registered Office: 342 Ladbroke Grove, London, W10 5BU
Parent: Fresh Trading Limited
Officers: James Lewis Davenport, Secretary; James Lewis Davenport [1973] Director and Company Secretary; Douglas Ross Lamont [1973] Director; Scott Edward Roche [1964] Director [Canadian]

Inside Armour Ltd
Incorporated: 2 January 2019
Registered Office: 61 Kelly Road, Hebburn, Tyne & Wear, NE31 2QN
Major Shareholder: Michael John Hobbs
Officers: Michael John Hobbs [1980] Director/Fitness Instructor

Iorange UK Limited
Incorporated: 30 October 2018
Registered Office: Flat 801, Jute Court, 58 Abbey Road, Barking, Essex, IG11 7FT
Officers: Olumolawa Oludotun Olusi [1977] Director [Nigerian]

Ipure Nutrition Limited
Incorporated: 27 March 2014 *Employees:* 1
Net Worth: £5,458 *Total Assets:* £56,968
Registered Office: 1st Floor, 311 Hale Road, Hale Barns, Altrincham, Cheshire, WA15 8SS
Major Shareholder: Ritu Chopra
Officers: Ritu Chopra [1978] Director

Islandgal Juice Ltd
Incorporated: 28 August 2018
Registered Office: Kemp House, 160 City Road, London, EC1V 2NX
Officers: Christina Daly [1992] Director/Business Owner [Irish]

J.T Freshly Limited
Incorporated: 24 May 2018
Registered Office: 59 North Downs Crescent, Croydon, Surrey, CR0 0LJ
Major Shareholder: Michael Cornerstone Onuh
Officers: Michael Cornerstone Onuh [1988] Director/Manager

Jamcan Ltd
Incorporated: 20 August 2018
Registered Office: 14 Stone Road, Bromley, Kent, BR2 9AU
Major Shareholder: Olivia Rochelle Simpson
Officers: Olivia Rochelle Simpson [1995] Director

Andrew M Jarvis Limited
Incorporated: 26 February 2013 *Employees:* 1
Net Worth: £11,163 *Total Assets:* £90,669
Registered Office: 34 Church Road, Flitcham, King's Lynn, Norfolk, PE31 6BU
Major Shareholder: Andrew Jarvis
Officers: Andrew Jarvis [1965] Director/Farming Contractor

JBC Juices Limited
Incorporated: 5 April 2017
Registered Office: 12 Helmet Row, London, EC1V 3QJ
Shareholders: Henry Little; George Stanley James Taylor
Officers: John Drain [1993] Director/Consultant; Henry Little [1983] Director/Teacher; George Stanley James Taylor [1988] Director/Editing Consultant

Judge Juice Ltd
Incorporated: 15 January 2018
Registered Office: 30 The Briars, Wool, Wareham, Dorset, BH20 6NA
Major Shareholder: Iain Donaldson
Officers: Iain Donaldson [1981] Director

Juice 1st Limited
Incorporated: 16 May 2016
Registered Office: 104 Woodbourne Avenue, Brighton, BN1 8EJ
Officers: Eloise Buswell, Secretary; Annette Buswell [1962] Director

Juice A Day Limited
Incorporated: 5 July 2016
Net Worth Deficit: £32,964 *Total Assets:* £39,529
Registered Office: Flat 8, The Grange, Holloway Drive, Virginia Park, Surrey, GU25 4ST
Shareholders: Parminder Panesar; Harrison James Spencer; Parminder Panesar; Harrison James Spencer
Officers: Parminder Panesar [1984] Director/Business Owner; Harrison James Spencer [1988] Director/Business Owner

Juice and Go Ltd
Incorporated: 20 March 2018
Registered Office: 409 Wandsworth Road, London, SW8 2JP
Major Shareholder: Sandor Komlosi
Officers: Sandor Komlosi [1988] Director [Hungarian]

Juice and Vegan Ltd
Incorporated: 13 August 2018
Registered Office: 2 Gathorne Road, London, N22 5ND
Officers: Ercumet Karakoc [1965] Director [Turkish]

Juice Delivery Service Ltd
Incorporated: 24 August 2018
Registered Office: 4 Devizes Road, Swindon, Wilts, SN1 4BJ
Major Shareholder: Krzysztof Stefan Talikowski
Officers: Krzysztof Stefan Talikowski [1982] Director/Businessman

The Juice Executive Ltd
Incorporated: 4 June 2014 *Employees:* 24
Net Worth Deficit: £263,239 *Total Assets:* £234,227
Registered Office: Unit 31 Revenge Road, Lordswood, Kent, ME5 8UD
Major Shareholder: Alexandra Frances Williams
Officers: Alexandra Frances Williams [1991] Director

Juice Fit JQ Limited
Incorporated: 10 February 2014 *Employees:* 2
Previous: Juice4u Ltd
Net Worth Deficit: £9,538 *Total Assets:* £1,848
Registered Office: 34-44 Northwood Street, Birmingham, B3 1TU
Major Shareholder: Cy Tunnicliff
Officers: Cy Tunnicliff [1975] Director/Fitness Trainer

Juice Freaks Co Ltd
Incorporated: 17 September 2018
Registered Office: 33 Cherrytree Gardens, Whitley Bay, Tyne & Wear, NE25 8XA
Major Shareholder: Denise Stutter
Officers: Denise Stutter [1966] Director

Juice Garden Limited
Incorporated: 22 October 2013
Registered Office: 181 Gravelly Hill, 10 Cedar Tree Court, Birmingham, B23 7NP
Major Shareholder: Darren Mark Henry
Officers: Darren Mark Henry [1976] Director/Manufacture of Fruit & Vegetable Juice

Juice HQ Ltd
Incorporated: 17 August 2018
Registered Office: 63 Springfield Gardens, Upminster, Essex, RM14 3EP
Shareholders: Katie Ann Thomas; Scott Jason Thomas
Officers: Katie Ann Thomas [1973] Marketing Director; Scott Jason Thomas [1971] Director/Production Manager

Juice Junkie London Limited
Incorporated: 9 November 2017
Registered Office: 68 Ulster Gardens, London, N13 5DW
Officers: Mahmut Dede [1983] Director

Juice Junkiez Limited
Incorporated: 13 October 2017
Registered Office: 100 Dartmouth Road, London, NW2 4HB
Officers: Jermaine Thompson [1986] Director

Juice Philosophy Limited
Incorporated: 20 January 2014
Net Worth Deficit: £49,908 *Total Assets:* £2,083
Registered Office: Suite 3, First Floor, The Hamilton Centre, Rodney Way, Chelmsford, Essex, CM1 3BY
Major Shareholder: Geeta Ann Foottit
Officers: Geeta Ann Foottit [1977] Director

The Juice Smith Limited
Incorporated: 17 March 2014
Net Worth Deficit: £603,554 *Total Assets:* £256,644
Registered Office: Winton Place, 16 Blackhills, Esher, Surrey, KT10 9JW
Major Shareholder: Richard Smith-Bernal
Officers: Graham Francis Smith [1958] Director; Richard Smith-Bernal [1989] Director/Personal Trainer

The Juice Tap Ltd
Incorporated: 25 July 2018
Registered Office: 20-22 Wenlock Road, London, N1 7GU
Major Shareholder: George Edward Brian Cope
Officers: George Edward Brian Cope [1993] Director/Farm Manager

The Juice Unit Ltd
Incorporated: 13 August 2018
Registered Office: 422 Brixton Road, London, SW9 7AE
Major Shareholder: Aron Kidane
Officers: Aron Kidane [1991] Director

The Juice Warrior Ltd
Incorporated: 6 February 2019
Registered Office: First Floor, Beaumont House, Lambton Road, London, SW20 0LW
Major Shareholder: Rachael Godinet
Officers: Rachael Godinet [1974] Director [British/New Zealander]

Juicebaby Ltd.
Incorporated: 11 March 2013 *Employees:* 32
Net Worth: £198,038 *Total Assets:* £532,755
Registered Office: 398 Kings Road, Chelsea, London, SW10 0LJ
Officers: Aida Foustok [1986] Director

Juiced Ltd
Incorporated: 6 July 2018
Registered Office: 592 Eastern Avenue, Ilford, Essex, IG2 6PQ
Shareholders: Neelam Potiwal; Neelam Wanti Potiwal
Officers: Neelam Wanti Potiwal [1986] Director/Entrepreneur

Juicee Beets Ltd
Incorporated: 31 October 2016
Net Worth Deficit: £5,435 *Total Assets:* £7,232
Registered Office: 34 School Lane, Manchester, M20 6RG
Major Shareholder: Amy Amy Oneill
Officers: Amy O'Neill [1984] Director

Juices on the Go Ltd
Incorporated: 30 January 2015
Net Worth: £464 *Total Assets:* £2,378
Registered Office: Demsa Accounts, 278 Langham Road, London, N15 3NP
Major Shareholder: Ilhan Abay
Officers: Ilhan Abay [1979] Director/Businessman [Turkish]

Juiceworks Limited
Incorporated: 29 May 2002
Net Worth: £2,650,789 *Total Assets:* £3,600,311
Registered Office: Sonex Works, 1934 Sharston Road, Wythenshawe, Manchester, M22 4RA
Shareholder: Crest Oil Holdings Limited
Officers: Tariq Sultan Ghani, Secretary; Abeda Rashid Ghani [1959] Director; Tariq Sultan Ghani [1955] Director

The Juicing Company Limited
Incorporated: 29 March 2017 *Employees:* 1
Net Worth Deficit: £4,925 *Total Assets:* £599
Registered Office: 4 Glenury Road, Stonehaven, Aberdeenshire, AB39 3LB
Shareholders: Vanessa Marianne Bremner; Vanessa Marianne Bremner
Officers: Stuart John Bremner [1982] Director; Vanessa Marianne Bremner [1991] Director

Juicyology Ltd
Incorporated: 13 December 2018
Registered Office: 87 The Lindens, New Addington, Croydon, Surrey, CR0 9EL
Major Shareholder: Natalie Marie-Colette Cafun
Officers: Natalie Marie-Colette Cafun [1979] Director/Graphic Designer

Karma Juice Ltd
Incorporated: 16 February 2015
Registered Office: 3 Avon Close, Calcot, Reading, Berks, RG31 7YE
Major Shareholder: James Oliver Clayton
Officers: James Oliver Clayton [1988] Director/Accountant

Karrmancooks Ltd
Incorporated: 27 April 2018
Registered Office: 119 Turton Road, Tipton, W Midlands, DY4 9LW
Major Shareholder: Karrman Patience Paurache
Officers: Karrman Patience Paurache [1991] Director

Kemetic Cooks Ltd
Incorporated: 11 January 2017
Registered Office: 52 Hardinge Crescent, London, SE18 6TB
Major Shareholder: Dwayne Thompson
Officers: Dwayne Thompson [1979] Director

Kleos Naturals Ltd
Incorporated: 10 July 2018
Registered Office: 20-22 Wenlock Road, London, N1 7GU
Major Shareholder: Enitan Adebola Femi-Obasan
Officers: Enitan Adebola Femi-Obasan [1980] Director [Nigerian]

Kunubu Ltd
Incorporated: 21 January 2019
Registered Office: Daren Isaf, Cwmyoy, Abergavenny, Monmouthshire, NP7 7NR
Shareholders: Peter Gavin Pinnock; Ian Hamilton
Officers: Ian Hamilton [1964] Creative Director; Peter Gavin Pinnock [1969] Director/Grower

LB Londom Ltd
Incorporated: 29 September 2018
Registered Office: 10 Main Road, Winterbourne Gunner, Salisbury, Wilts, SP4 6EE
Major Shareholder: Wendy Diana Stevens

Lemony Drinks Ltd
Incorporated: 27 July 2016
Previous: Ooze Drinks Ltd
Net Worth Deficit: £5,370 *Total Assets:* £1,059
Registered Office: Barking Enterprise Centre, Cambridge Road, Barking, Essex, IG11 8FG
Shareholder: Giuseppe Baidoo
Officers: Giuseppe Baidoo [1990] Director/Entrepreneur [Italian]

Liberty Orchards Limited
Incorporated: 22 April 2010 *Employees:* 3
Net Worth Deficit: £16,554 *Total Assets:* £169,754
Registered Office: 14 Fairmont Terrace, Sherborne, Dorset, DT9 3JS
Officers: Robert Francis Imlach [1953] Director/Business Owner; Alison Jean Lemmey [1963] Director/Speech Therapist; Peter John Lemmey [1962] Director/Farmer; Victoria Morland [1965] Director/Publishing Manager

Little Stour Orchard Ltd
Incorporated: 8 February 2011
Registered Office: Uprising, Shottendane Road, Margate, Kent, CT9 4NE
Officers: Clifford Roffey, Secretary; Michael David Bowers [1964] Director/Apple Farmer/Cider Maker; Dr Sarah Jane Bowers [1968] Senior Director

Little Teapot Ltd
Incorporated: 18 September 2018
Registered Office: 5 Kingsley Grove, Audenshaw, Manchester, M34 5GT
Major Shareholder: James Robert Whewell
Officers: James Robert Whewell [1980] Director

Livewheatgrass Limited
Incorporated: 28 May 2009 *Employees:* 9
Net Worth: £266,635 *Total Assets:* £305,562
Registered Office: 25 High Street, Gretton, Corby, Northants, NN17 3DE
Shareholders: Daniel Piec; Britt Cordi Piec
Officers: Dr Britt Cordi-Piec [1966] Director/Nature Conservationist [Danish]

Livitus Limited
Incorporated: 27 December 2017
Registered Office: 2 St Philips Place, Birmingham, B3 2RB
Shareholders: Oyedele Abidemi Olaoye; Thomas Aymen Jabrane
Officers: Dr Thomas Aymen Jabrane [1982] Director/Entrepreneur [French]; Oyedele Abidemi Olaoye [1985] Director/Entrepreneur

Love Skin Company Ltd
Incorporated: 21 March 2018
Registered Office: 157 Silver Street, London, N18 1PY
Major Shareholder: Chardonay Chardonay Clarke
Officers: Chardonay Clarke [1993] Director

Love Yourself UK Limited
Incorporated: 23 September 2015
Net Worth Deficit: £582 *Total Assets:* £6,600
Registered Office: 570 Kingston Road, Raynes Park, London, SW20 8DR
Major Shareholder: Andrea Okos
Officers: Andrea Agota Okos [1970] Director/Natural Juice Therapist and Colonic Hydro-Therapist [Hungarian]

LSG PVT Ltd
Incorporated: 10 September 2018
Registered Office: Kemp House, 160 City Road, London, EC1V 2NX
Major Shareholder: Dumiso Harahwa
Officers: Dumiso Harahwa, Secretary; Dumiso Harahwa [1966] Director/Self Employed

Lytegro Limited
Incorporated: 8 April 2015
Net Worth Deficit: £38,896 *Total Assets:* £32,102
Registered Office: Dock 108, 75 Exploration Drive, Leicester, LE4 5NU
Shareholders: Andrew Lee; Mark Lyte
Officers: Andrew John Lee, Secretary; Dr Andrew John Lee [1970] Director/Business Development Manager; Mark Lyte [1954] Director/Lecturer [American]

McBerries Ltd
Incorporated: 4 December 2018
Registered Office: Sterling House, 3 Wavell Drive, Rosehill Industrial Estate, Carlisle, Cumbria, CA1 2SA
Major Shareholder: Ryan James McPherson
Officers: Ryan James McPherson [1988] Director

Mebifarm Ltd
Incorporated: 15 December 2017
Registered Office: 183-189 The Vale, London, W3 7RW
Major Shareholder: Ali Adnan
Officers: Ali Adnan [1967] Director

MG International Trading UK Limited
Incorporated: 21 August 2015
Registered Office: No 1 Cochrane House, Admirals Way, Canary Wharf, London, E14 9UD
Shareholders: Karim Marghany Elsayed Marghany; Ahmad Marghany Elsayed Marghany
Officers: Karim Marghany Elsayed Marghany [1976] Director [Egyptian]

Mobie Corporation Limited
Incorporated: 1 March 2013
Net Worth: £635 *Total Assets:* £800
Registered Office: 37 Farningham Road, London, N17 0PP
Major Shareholder: Emmanuel Chinonye Obi
Officers: Emmanuel Chinonye Obi [1972] Director

Muscle in Motion Ltd
Incorporated: 19 February 2019
Registered Office: 90a Chamberlayne Road, London, NW10 3JL
Officers: Michael Martin [1974] Director/Personal Trainer and Massage Therapist

My Goodness (British Farmers) Ltd
Incorporated: 24 January 2019
Registered Office: Barnes Roffe LLP, Charles Lake House, Claire Causeway, Crossways Business Park, Dartford, Kent, DA2 6QA
Shareholders: Philip John Acock; David Leonard Hall
Officers: Philip John Acock [1963] Managing Director

My Monkey Doesn't Like Bananas Anymore Ltd
Incorporated: 15 May 2018
Registered Office: 43 Lancaster Gate, London, W2 3NA
Officers: Samuel Owen [1996] Director/General Manager

The Naked Juice Company Ltd
Incorporated: 23 March 2015
Net Worth: £1 *Total Assets:* £1
Registered Office: 6 Lower Calderbrook, Littleborough, Lancs, OL15 9HL
Shareholder: Wayne Redmond
Officers: Lisa Camps [1983] Director; Wayne Redman [1967] Director

Nattyroots Ital Juice Limited
Incorporated: 2 January 2019
Registered Office: The Gatehouse, De Bradelei House, Chapel Street, Belper, Derbys, DE56 1AR
Shareholders: Silbert Blackwood; Ruel Levi Duncan
Officers: Ruel Levi Duncan, Secretary; Silbert Blackwood [1950] Director; Ruel Levi Duncan [1948] Director

Natural CBD Solutions Ltd
Incorporated: 7 February 2019
Registered Office: 133 Asgard Drive, Salford, M5 4TG
Major Shareholder: Damien Paul Jordan
Officers: Damien Paul Jordan [1988] Director/Consultant

Naturally Ugly Ltd
Incorporated: 5 March 2018
Registered Office: 6/1 Haddon's Court, Edinburgh, EH8 9EL
Parent: Naturally Ugly
Officers: Rory McDonald [1995] Director/Banking

Natvitanet Ltd
Incorporated: 23 July 2015
Net Worth: £1,776 *Total Assets:* £2,255
Registered Office: 77 High Street, Littlehampton, W Sussex, BN17 5AG
Shareholders: Peter Cserveni; Gabriella Kovacs
Officers: Peter Zoltan Cserveni [1962] Director [Hungarian]; Gabriella Kovacs [1984] Director [Hungarian]

Neacsu Construct Ltd
Incorporated: 12 November 2018
Registered Office: Flat A, 206 Valley Road, London, SW16 2AE
Major Shareholder: Ovidiu Neacsu
Officers: Ovidiu Neacsu [1989] Director [Romanian]

Neema Food Ltd
Incorporated: 9 September 2015
Net Worth Deficit: £34,597 *Total Assets:* £633
Registered Office: 3 Ching Way, London, E4 8YD
Officers: Yohari Kasongo [1964] Director/Nurse; Rose Mauwa Yombo-Djema [1984] Director/Fundraising Manager

Neptune SA Ltd
Incorporated: 12 March 2018
Registered Office: Mays Grove Cottage, Mays Lane, Dedham, Colchester, Essex, CO7 6EW
Officers: Antanas Sadauskas [1965] Director [Lithuanian]

Never Not Natural Ltd
Incorporated: 26 March 2018
Registered Office: 18 Sidenhill Close, Shirley, Solihull, W Midlands, B90 2QD
Major Shareholder: Adam Silvanus Ward
Officers: Adam Silvanus Ward [1993] Director

Nourish Juice Ltd
Incorporated: 22 February 2016
Registered Office: 74 West Bar Street, Banbury, Oxon, OX16 9RZ
Officers: Ayesha Ali [1986] Director/Yoga Teacher

Odopa Foods Ltd
Incorporated: 3 August 2018
Registered Office: The Well, 50 Coverdale Crescent, Manchester, M12 4FG
Major Shareholder: Abena Agyeman
Officers: Abena Agyeman [1963] Director and Company Secretary

Olives Britannia Foreign Trade Co. Ltd
Incorporated: 30 August 2018
Registered Office: 3rd Floor, 86-90 Paul Street, London, EC2A 4NE
Major Shareholder: Erdinc Selvi
Officers: Erdinc Selvi [1955] Director [Turkish]

Oliviccio Ltd
Incorporated: 29 November 2007 *Employees:* 2
Net Worth Deficit: £11,038 *Total Assets:* £13,683
Registered Office: 108 Wallhill Road, Dobcross, Oldham, Lancs, OL3 5BH
Shareholders: Carl Woodhead; Nicola Jane Hill
Officers: Carl Woodhead, Secretary; Nikki Hill [1964] Director/Graphic Designer; Carl Woodhead [1963] Director/Project Manager

One54 Holdings Ltd
Incorporated: 17 September 2015
Net Worth: £198,015 *Total Assets:* £216,819
Registered Office: 3rd Floor, 114a Cromwell Road, London, SW7 4AG
Major Shareholder: Henry Hickman Bacon
Officers: Nicholas Leigh Ackerman [1986] Director [Irish]; Henry Hickman Bacon [1984] Director; Andrew Adinorte Boye Doe [1956] Director [Ghanaian]; Charles David Courtney Comyn [1977] Director/Consultant; William Robert Falconer [1988] Director

Onion Jo Limited
Incorporated: 27 November 2014
Net Worth: £46,033 *Total Assets:* £46,040
Registered Office: Merton House, Merton, Okehampton, Devon, EX20 3DS
Shareholders: Philip William Baker; Reginald Robert Key
Officers: Philip William Baker [1961] Director/Food Wholesaler

Orchard Blossoms Limited
Incorporated: 9 July 2018
Registered Office: 2 Genever Close, London, E4 9BT
Shareholders: Naila Mir; Tabassum Mir; Sierra Mir
Officers: Naila Mir [1978] Director and Company Secretary; Sierra Mir [1980] Director; Tabassum Mir [1985] Director

Orchard House Foods Limited
Incorporated: 21 March 1985 *Employees:* 1,205
Net Worth: £7,621,000 *Total Assets:* £47,484,000
Registered Office: 79 Manton Road, Earlstrees Industrial Estate, Corby, Northants, NN17 4JL
Parent: Hain Frozen Foods UK Limited
Officers: Nick Keen, Secretary; Denise Menikheim Faltischek [1973] Director/Attorney [American]; James Michael Langrock [1965] Director [American]; Mark Lawrence Schiller [1961] Director/CEO Hain Celestial [American]; Robin James Skidmore [1968] Director

Orchard Origins C.I.C.
Incorporated: 15 December 2014
Registered Office: Queenswood Country Park, Dinmore Hill, Leominster, Herefords, HR6 0PY
Parent: Herefordshire Wildlife Trust
Officers: Peter James Ford [1955] Director/Retired; Laurence John Green [1977] Director/Manager; Brian Peter Robert Hurrell [1943] Director; Sally Jane Pike [1957] Director; Adrian Wilcox [1951] Director/Social Work

The Oxford Juice Company Ltd
Incorporated: 9 May 2018
Registered Office: 34 Victor Street, Oxford, OX2 6BT
Shareholders: Sphelo Sphephelo Skhumbuzo Madlala; Akeem Trinity Perry Williams
Officers: Akeem Trinity Perry Williams, Secretary; Sphelo Sphephelo Skhumbuzo Madlala [1989] Director/Manager [South African]

PAS Engineering Limited
Incorporated: 3 July 2002
Net Worth: £11,966 *Total Assets:* £22,154
Registered Office: Fell View, Browhouses, Eastriggs, Annan, Dumfries, DG12 6TG
Officers: Paul Anthony Sparrow, Secretary/Engineer; Miriam Hazel Sparrow [1957] Director/Office Clerk; Paul Anthony Sparrow [1957] Director/Engineer

Passion 4 Juice Limited
Incorporated: 13 May 2003
Net Worth: £4,061 *Total Assets:* £86,265
Registered Office: Trullwell, Box, Stroud, Glos, GL6 9HD
Major Shareholder: Patricia Margaret Tucker
Officers: Joseph Piers Cecil May, Secretary; Joseph Piers Cecil May [1967] Director; Patricia Margaret Tucker [1969] Managing Director [Australian]

Pastel D'Nata Ltd.
Incorporated: 12 February 2018
Registered Office: Flat 4, Parkview, 16 Braidley Road, Bournemouth, BH2 6JX
Major Shareholder: Rafael Alexandre Pires Martins
Officers: Rafael Alexandre Pires Martins [1988] Director/Web Developer [Portuguese]

Perfect Brands (Europe) Limited
Incorporated: 3 August 2017
Registered Office: c/o N M Shah & Company, Miller House, Rosslyn Crescent, Harrow, Middlesex, HA1 2RZ
Shareholders: Rajesh Dattani; Sanjay Dattani
Officers: Rajesh Dattani [1958] Director; Sanjay Dattani [1962] Director

Perfect Brands Ltd
Incorporated: 20 September 2017
Registered Office: c/o N M Shah & Company, Miller House, Rosslyn Crescent, Harrow, Middlesex, HA1 2RZ
Officers: Rajesh Dattani [1958] Director; Sanjay Dattani [1962] Director

Martina Peters Ltd
Incorporated: 11 June 2014
Net Worth: £1 *Total Assets:* £1
Registered Office: 18 Cedar House, Cedar Tree Grove, London, SE27 0QD
Major Shareholder: Marta Pietkiewicz
Officers: Marta Pietkiewicz [1983] Director [Polish]

PG Foods Ltd
Incorporated: 12 June 2013
Registered Office: 20-22 Wenlock Road, London, N1 7GU
Parent: Gourmet Ventures Group Ltd
Officers: Raj Singhal [1971] Director/Businessman

Phoenexus Ltd
Incorporated: 27 April 2018
Registered Office: 129 Burnley Road, Padiham, Burnley, Lancs, BB12 8BA
Shareholders: Garry Farparan; Emma Jones
Officers: Garry Farparan [1973] Director [Filipino]

The Pickle House Limited
Incorporated: 14 August 2017 *Employees:* 1
Net Worth: £18,889 *Total Assets:* £26,646
Registered Office: 21 St Jude Street, London, N16 8JU
Major Shareholder: Florence Agnes Coco Cherruault
Officers: Florence Agnes Coco Cherruault [1990] Director

Pixley Berries (Juice) Limited
Incorporated: 17 January 2007 *Employees:* 14
Net Worth: £735,004 *Total Assets:* £2,325,956
Registered Office: Poolend, Pixley, Ledbury, Herefords, HR8 2RB
Major Shareholder: Edward Ballard Thompson
Officers: Hannah Mary Parker, Secretary; Edward Ballard Thompson [1944] Director/Farmer

Plenish Cleanse Ltd
Incorporated: 20 June 2012 *Employees:* 14
Net Worth: £224,260 *Total Assets:* £1,647,191
Registered Office: Unit 24, W10 Studios, 2-4 Exmoor Street, London, W10 6BD
Shareholders: Pembroke VCT; Kara Rosen
Officers: Leon Edward Diamond [1977] Director [Australian]; Brian Maloney [1969] Director; Kara Rosen [1977] Director [American]; Andrew Daniel Wolfson [1969] Director

Pome de Vita Limited
Incorporated: 13 May 2013
Registered Office: 3 Fleet Close, Hughenden Valley, High Wycombe, Bucks, HP14 4LL
Officers: Tulin Lester [1969] Director

Presse Limited
Incorporated: 7 April 2017
Net Worth: £20,125 *Total Assets:* £31,885
Registered Office: 3rd Floor, 86-90 Paul Street, London, EC2A 4NE
Major Shareholder: Tua Christiansson
Officers: Tua Christiansson, Secretary; Tua Christiansson [1976] Director [Finnish]

Pressed Ltd
Incorporated: 22 October 2018
Registered Office: 56 Beechwood Avenue, Thornton Heath, Surrey, CR7 7DZ
Major Shareholder: Melissa Michelle Morris
Officers: Melissa Michelle Morris [1988] Director

Prickly Pear Potion Ltd
Incorporated: 17 September 2018
Registered Office: Flat 8, 1 Douro Street, London, E3 2TS
Major Shareholder: Mohammed Sobur Khan
Officers: Mohammed Sobur Khan [1983] Director/Analyst

The Proper Protein Company Ltd.
Incorporated: 7 February 2018
Registered Office: 156 Stretford Road, Urmston, Manchester, M41 9LT
Major Shareholder: Jordan Karl Street
Officers: Jordan Karl Street [1996] Director/Founder

Pura Pressed Ltd
Incorporated: 29 January 2016 *Employees:* 2
Net Worth Deficit: £12,202 *Total Assets:* £12,334
Registered Office: 2 St George's Hill, Perranporth, Cornwall, TR6 0LE
Shareholder: Graeme Holland
Officers: Ronald Albert William Holland, Secretary; Graeme Holland [1981] Director

Pure Press Ltd
Incorporated: 30 August 2016
Registered Office: Flat 5, 11 Wallace Gardens, Edinburgh, EH12 6HT
Officers: Jordan Robertson [1985] Director

Purer Ltd
Incorporated: 11 December 2017
Registered Office: 18 Avoca Court, 146 Cheapside, Birmingham, B12 0PR
Major Shareholder: Max Lucas
Officers: Max Lucas, Secretary; Max Lucas [1989] Director

Purity Organic Juice Ltd
Incorporated: 4 February 2019
Registered Office: 20 Peakdale Avenue, Crumpsall, Manchester, M8 5QB
Shareholders: Yindula Bokolombe Emilie Konde; David Msughter Ageba
Officers: David Msughter Ageba [1984] Director/IT Consultant [Nigerian]; Yindula Bokolombe Emilie Konde [1995] Director/Carer [Swiss]

Rafiq Costcutter Limited
Incorporated: 16 May 2018
Registered Office: 38 Laindon Road, Manchester, M14 5DP
Major Shareholder: Rafiq Ahmad
Officers: Rafiq Ahmad [1991] Director [Pakistani]

Raw Candy Ltd
Incorporated: 8 March 2018
Registered Office: 102 Victor Road, Middlesex, Teddington, Middlesex, TW11 3AS
Officers: Phoebe Middleton, Secretary; Sophie Ann Middleton [1980] Director/Designer

Raw Cure Limited
Incorporated: 2 April 2015
Registered Office: 12 Scotchmen Close, Minster on Sea, Sheerness, Kent, ME12 3BX
Major Shareholder: Ben Callum Staples
Officers: Ben Callum Staples [1986] Director/Nutrition

Rawness Limited
Incorporated: 4 April 2017
Registered Office: 126 Chinnor Crescent, Greenford, Middlesex, UB6 9NY
Major Shareholder: Robert Marek Sak
Officers: Robert Marek Sak [1967] Director [Polish]

Rayner and Rooster Limited
Incorporated: 7 February 2019
Registered Office: Yew Tree House, The Shrubbery, Church Street, St Neots, Cambs, PE19 2BU
Shareholders: Rebecca Eve Rayner; Philip John Rayner
Officers: Philip John Rayner [1973] Director; Rebecca Eve Rayner [1970] Director

Razoo Limited
Incorporated: 30 July 2015
Net Worth Deficit: £9,062 *Total Assets:* £292
Registered Office: Lower Ground Floor, 40 Bloomsbury Way, London, WC1A 2SE
Shareholders: Andrew James Darragh Field; Rosheeka Dilhani Amarasekara Field
Officers: Andrew James Darragh Field [1980] Director [Australian]; Rosheeka Dilhani Amarasekara Field [1981] Director [Australian]

Ready Steady Glow London Limited
Incorporated: 25 July 2016
Registered Office: 4 Cornwall Crescent, London, W11 1PP
Major Shareholder: Yasmine Cherquaoui
Officers: Yasmine Cherquaoui [1979] Director

Real Shhh Limited
Incorporated: 5 June 2017
Registered Office: 53 Alric Avenue, London, NW10 8RA
Shareholder: Michelle Johnson
Officers: Michelle Johnson [1988] Director

Realdrink Ltd
Incorporated: 3 August 2009
Net Worth Deficit: £1,508 *Total Assets:* £20,605
Registered Office: Beverley Court, Upton Manor Road, St Marys, Brixham, Devon, TQ5 9RG
Officers: Annabel Charlotte Akeroyd [1969] Director/Drinks Manufacturer; Simon Andrew Akeroyd [1973] Director

The Refreshing Drinks Company Limited
Incorporated: 21 February 2019
Registered Office: Kemp House, 160 City Road, London, EC1V 2NX
Officers: Simon Galea, Secretary; Paul Archard [1964] Director; Aneil Bedi [1967] Director; Simon David Galea [1961] Director; Taner Ozsumer [1986] Director

Rejuce Limited
Incorporated: 5 April 2017
Registered Office: Unit 1a, 10 Stour Road, Vittoria Wharf, Stour Road, London, E3 2NT
Major Shareholder: Thomas Fletcher
Officers: Thomas Fletcher [1987] Director

Rejuveu Ltd
Incorporated: 29 May 2018
Registered Office: 4 Rustic Avenue, Tooting, London, SW16 6PD
Shareholders: Cynthia Patricia Young; Lourn Hugh Foster
Officers: Cynthia Patricia Young [1955] Director/Headmistress

Restore Juice Company Limited
Incorporated: 8 March 2016
Net Worth Deficit: £3,645 *Total Assets:* £530
Registered Office: Treetops, Mill Lane, Willaston, Neston, Wirral, Merseyside, CH64 1RF
Shareholders: Joanne Willcox; Kendal Elizabeth Williams-McKean
Officers: Joanne Willcox, Secretary; Joanne Willcox [1965] Director; Kendal Elizabeth Williams-McKean [1985] Director

Revive Us Limited
Incorporated: 30 August 2017
Registered Office: Flat 2, 189 Holdenhurst Road, Bournemouth, BH8 8DG
Officers: Christopher Pane [1988] Director

Rhythm Health Limited
Incorporated: 26 February 2014 *Employees:* 2
Net Worth Deficit: £168,378 *Total Assets:* £172,171
Registered Office: 12 Hatherley Road, Sidcup, Kent, DA14 4DT
Shareholders: Brian Owens; Patrick James Tobin
Officers: Brian Owens [1963] Director; Patrick James Tobin [1951] Director

Rootyfruit Limited
Incorporated: 15 October 2018
Registered Office: 313 Woodstock Road, Oxford, OX2 7NY
Shareholders: Lucy Conchita Channer; Caroline Slootweg
Officers: Lucy Conchita Channer [1975] Director/Founder; Caroline Slootweg [1975] Director/Co Founder [Dutch]

Rose and Gold Drinks Limited
Incorporated: 28 June 2016
Registered Office: 18 Cyprus Road, London, N3 3RY
Major Shareholder: Christine Sarah Lynskey
Officers: Christine Sarah Lynskey [1984] Director

Rosehip Farms Limited
Incorporated: 22 September 2017
Net Worth: £100 *Total Assets:* £7,673
Registered Office: Clarendon House, 42 Clarence Street, Cheltenham, Glos, GL50 3PL
Major Shareholder: Rikki Alice Burford
Officers: Michael Burford [1988] Director; Dr Rikki Alice Burford [1988] Director/Veterinary Surgeon

Route 33 Limited
Incorporated: 11 October 2017
Registered Office: 37 Warren Street, London, W1T 6AD
Shareholders: Warren Douglas Pole; Erica Emily Eva Pole
Officers: Daniel Jeffery Lameire [1969] Director/Consultant [Canadian]; Erica Emily Eva Pole [1970] Director; Warren Douglas Pole [1973] Director

Seabuckthorn Scotland Community Interest Company
Incorporated: 17 December 2018
Registered Office: 45/2 East Claremont Street, Edinburgh, EH7 4HU
Officers: Kirstie Eira Campbell [1978] Director/Humanitarian Aid Consultant; Roberto Nicholas Granozio [1988] Director/Territory Manager; Lorna Ruth Kelly [1977] Director/Investor Relations Manager

Selva Group Limited
Incorporated: 12 July 2018
Registered Office: No 1 Royal Exchange, London, EC3V 3DG
Major Shareholder: Mateo Akira Notsuke Gonzalez
Officers: Mateo Akira Notsuke Gonzalez [1994] Director [Spanish]

The Simply Great Drinks (Europe) Limited
Incorporated: 6 May 2014 *Employees:* 3
Net Worth: £11,242 *Total Assets:* £219,396
Registered Office: 61 MacRae Road, Ham Green, Bristol, BS20 0DD
Major Shareholder: Professor Colin Gordon Turner

Sinful Foods Limited
Incorporated: 18 June 2007
Registered Office: Unit 7 Woodhill Park, Old Dalby, Leicester, LE14 3LX
Major Shareholder: Richard Dean Ledger
Officers: Richard Dean Ledger [1966] Director

Smartervites Ltd
Incorporated: 4 March 2015
Net Worth Deficit: £14,068 *Total Assets:* £100
Registered Office: 69 Viking, Bracknell, Berks, RG12 8UN
Major Shareholder: Glenn Wheeler
Officers: Glenn Wheeler [1964] Director/Nutrition Industry

Smoofeez Limited
Incorporated: 29 September 2017
Registered Office: 76 Brunswick Street, Derby, DE23 8TQ
Major Shareholder: Ross Archer
Officers: Ross Archer [1994] Director/Founder

Snowdonia Birch Water Ltd
Incorporated: 26 October 2018
Registered Office: Caeaddawyn, Rhydymain, Dolgellau, Gwynedd, LL40 2BU
Major Shareholder: Mike Edwards
Officers: Mike Edwards [1988] Director

E & M Soroka Ltd
Incorporated: 5 February 2014
Net Worth: £16,789 *Total Assets:* £21,345
Registered Office: 55 Stanworth Avenue, Bolton, Lancs, BL2 6EW
Shareholder: Ewa Stanislawa Soroka
Officers: Ewa Stanislawa Soroka [1982] Director [Polish]; Michal Soroka [1985] Director [Polish]

Spider Cider Ltd
Incorporated: 16 November 2015
Previous: The Squeaky Shoe Company Ltd
Net Worth: £1 *Total Assets:* £1
Registered Office: Salisbury Cottage, St Brides Road, Caldicot, Gwent, NP26 3BB
Officers: Daniel Dyer [1976] Managing Director

Spnet Ltd.
Incorporated: 27 September 2013
Registered Office: Flat 10, Rockford House, 34-38 Heathcoat Street, Nottingham, NG1 3AA
Officers: Jorge Lorenzana, Secretary; Javier Castaneda [1986] Director/Politician [Spanish]; Miguel Castaneda [1983] Director/Consulting [Spanish]

Sprosen Accounts Ltd
Incorporated: 3 October 2017
Registered Office: 71-75 Shelton Street, London, WC2H 9JQ
Major Shareholder: Werner de Bruin
Officers: Werner de Bruin [1978] Director/Chief Executive Officer

SRAM & MRAM Limited
Incorporated: 5 February 2016
Registered Office: Suite 602, 26 Cheering Lane, East Village, Stratford, London, E20 1BD
Major Shareholder: Balasubramanian Seetharaman
Officers: Mary Mam [1987] Director [Cambodian]; Balasubramanian Seetharaman [1965] Director

SRAM & MRAM Technologies and Resources Limited
Incorporated: 23 December 2016
Registered Office: Lomond Court, Castle Business Park, Stirling, FK9 4TU
Major Shareholder: Sailesh Lachu Hiranandani
Officers: Mary Mam, Secretary; Mary Mam [1987] Director [Cambodian]; Balasubramanian Seetharaman [1965] Director

Stamford Juice Company Limited
Incorporated: 18 January 2002
Registered Office: 7 Emlyns Street, Stamford, Lincs, PE9 1QP
Major Shareholder: Nichola Keeble
Officers: Nichola Jane Keeble, Secretary; Richard John Keeble [1961] Director/Consultant

Straight Up Zesty Ltd.
Incorporated: 23 January 2019
Registered Office: 31 Laleham House, Camlet Street, London, E2 7HE
Shareholder: Verena Mengis
Officers: Verena Mengis [1999] Director/Student [German]

Strive Products Sco Limited
Incorporated: 15 January 2019
Registered Office: 41 Tinto Road, Glasgow, G43 2AH
Major Shareholder: Gordon James Belch
Officers: Gordon James Belch [1992] Director/Accountant

Suda Green REV Investment Limited
Incorporated: 13 February 2018
Registered Office: Flat B, 122 Camden Road, London, NW1 9EE
Officers: Abdalla Hussain Abdalla [1969] Director [German]

Sundance Partners Limited
Incorporated: 5 September 2008 *Employees:* 69
Previous: Hofmann Industries Limited
Net Worth: £4,877,415 *Total Assets:* £6,418,852
Registered Office: Units B35 to B39, New Covent Garden Market, Nine Elms, London, SW8 5HH
Shareholders: Patrick Hamilkar Hofmann; Sonmi Kim
Officers: Patrick Hamilkar Hofmann [1973] Director [German]; Sonmi Kim [1972] Director

Sunlife Organics Limited
Incorporated: 28 August 2018
Registered Office: 21 Birr Road, Bradford, BD9 4PQ
Major Shareholder: Omar Fayyaz
Officers: Omar Fayyaz [1990] Director

Sunrise Produce Ltd
Incorporated: 12 December 2009
Net Worth: £58,824 *Total Assets:* £352,030
Registered Office: 16a Well Street, Thetford, Norfolk, IP24 2BL
Shareholders: Devinder Kaur Randhawa; Kuldip Singh Randhawa
Officers: Davinder Kaur Randhawa [1978] Director; Kuldip Singh Randhawa [1980] Director [Indian]

Suppers Ready Limited
Incorporated: 10 April 2014
Net Worth: £5 *Total Assets:* £5
Registered Office: 8 Woodland View, Woodmancote, Cirencester, Glos, GL7 7DS
Major Shareholder: Andrew John Parffrey
Officers: Andrew Parffrey, Secretary; Andrew Parffrey [1955] Director/Restaurateur

SVZ (UK) Limited
Incorporated: 12 May 1988
Net Worth Deficit: £239,944
Registered Office: 31 Lee View, Enfield, Middlesex, EN2 8RY
Parent: SVZ Industrial Products BV
Officers: Anouk Ter Laak, Secretary; Anouk Ter Laak [1966] Director/Chief Executive [Dutch]

Sweet Palm Ltd
Incorporated: 19 March 2018
Registered Office: 55 Tarbert Walk, London, E1 0EE
Major Shareholder: Jewel Chowdhury
Officers: Jewel Chowdhury [1990] Director

Tam Events & Cafe Ltd
Incorporated: 3 August 2018
Registered Office: 33 Rockingham Road, Uxbridge, Middlesex, UB8 2TZ
Officers: Priya Coelho [1979] Director [Portuguese]

That Healthy Way Limited
Incorporated: 16 December 2014
Registered Office: 32 Magnolia Way, Cheshunt, Waltham Cross, Herts, EN8 0FD
Major Shareholder: Natalee Pringle
Officers: Natalee Pringle [1982] Director

Thornton Nurseries Ltd
Incorporated: 17 February 2011 *Employees:* 4
Net Worth Deficit: £3,341 *Total Assets:* £48,945
Registered Office: Temple Chambers, 16a Belvoir Road, Coalville, Leics, LE67 3QE
Major Shareholder: David John Smith
Officers: Susan Smith, Secretary; Benjamin David Smith [1984] Director/Nursery Administrator; David John Smith [1957] Director/Nursery Administrator; John William Smith [1931] Director

Tiddly Pommes Ltd
Incorporated: 17 October 2016
Net Worth: £33,965 *Total Assets:* £80,733
Registered Office: 6 London Place, Oxford, OX4 1BD
Major Shareholder: Rupert Ivor James Griffin
Officers: Hannah Clare Fenton [1983] Director/Marketing and Sales; Rupert Ivor James Griffin [1971] Director/Fruit Juice Manufacturer; Antony Richard David Melville [1952] Director/Publisher (Retired)

Tower Nursery Limited
Incorporated: 4 December 2013
Net Worth: £359,808 *Total Assets:* £1,526,129
Registered Office: c/o Mazars LLP, The Pinnacle, 160 Midsummer Boulevard, Milton Keynes, Bucks, MK9 1FF
Shareholder: Calogera Colletti
Officers: Giuseppe Colletti [1975] Director; Domenica Maniscalco [1971] Director

Trim and Trendy Limited
Incorporated: 19 July 2004
Net Worth: £142,870 *Total Assets:* £142,870
Registered Office: 31 Dennis Road, Kempston, Bedford, MK42 7HG
Major Shareholder: Sunday Adeniyi
Officers: Sunday Adeniyi [1970] Director

Trove International Limited
Incorporated: 7 December 2015
Registered Office: 3rd Floor, Cavendish House, 18 Cavendish Square, London, W1G 0PJ
Officers: Emeraba Afaoma Tony-Uzoebo [1974] Director/Accountant

Truth Tonics Limited
Incorporated: 26 March 2018
Registered Office: Adebeck House, Catton, Thirsk, N Yorks, YO7 4SQ
Shareholders: Rebecca Potter; Sally Harding
Officers: Rebecca Potter, Secretary; Sally Harding [1976] Director; Rebecca Potter [1984] Director

UK Dorset Ltd
Incorporated: 5 May 2017
Registered Office: 71-75 Shelton Street, Covent Garden, London, WC2H 9JQ
Major Shareholder: Saidabror Gulyamov
Officers: Shamagdiev Abdurasul [1987] Director [Uzbek]

Ultimate Juice Limited
Incorporated: 5 May 2016 *Employees:* 3
Net Worth Deficit: £42,011 *Total Assets:* £164,090
Registered Office: Desai & Co Accountants, Desai House, 9-13 Holbrook Lane, Coventry, Warwicks, CV6 4AD
Shareholder: Rodrigo Guillermo Emilio Hernandez
Officers: Rodrigo Guillermo Emilio Hernandez [1967] Director/Manager

Umoba Ltd
Incorporated: 6 October 2015
Registered Office: 52 Brackens Drive, Brentwood, Essex, CM14 5UE
Shareholders: Julie Thorogood; Rinni Embrechts
Officers: Rinni Embrechts [1987] Director [Belgian]

Urban Juice Ltd
Incorporated: 17 January 2014
Registered Office: 35 Woodstock Road, London, W4 1DS
Major Shareholder: Nicholas Ian Macdonald Mackintosh
Officers: Nicholas Ian Macdonald Mackintosh [1955] Director

Vegan Monster Ltd
Incorporated: 6 June 2018
Registered Office: 67 Newlands Drive, Forest Town, Mansfield, Notts, NG19 0HY
Major Shareholder: Buddy Lee
Officers: Buddy Lee [1989] Director

Vegishake Ltd
Incorporated: 9 September 2015
Net Worth Deficit: £12,031 *Total Assets:* £2,292
Registered Office: Suite AM, 104 Boleyn House, 776-778 Barking Road, London, E13 9PJ
Major Shareholder: Michael Van-Dongen
Officers: Michael Van-Dongen [1989] Director

Verjuice Limited
Incorporated: 30 July 2015
Net Worth: £100 *Total Assets:* £100
Registered Office: 63 High Street, Hurstpierpoint, W Sussex, BN6 9RE
Shareholder: Antony Richard Cozzi
Officers: Antony Richard Cozzi [1960] Director; Carole May Guotavia Cozzi [1961] Director

The Vitsuk Ltd
Incorporated: 4 December 2017
Registered Office: Flat 1, Blandford House, Richborne Terrace, London, SW8 1LB
Officers: Ilerika Jamie Oluwayomi Bolarinwa [1987] Director/Shop Assistant

W & W Drinks Ltd
Incorporated: 9 January 2019
Registered Office: Unit 2 Broadview Farm, The Ridge, Cold Ash, Thatcham, Berks, RG18 9HX
Shareholders: Gary Christopher Wickens; Richard Anthony Wyatt
Officers: Gary Christopher Wickens [1977] Director; Richard Anthony Wyatt [1977] Director

Wasted Apple Co Ltd
Incorporated: 14 November 2014
Net Worth Deficit: £3,346 *Total Assets:* £5,265
Registered Office: Southwinds, Porthpean Beach Road, St Austell, Cornwall, PL26 6AU
Officers: Mark Andrew Rudge [1969] Director/Local Government

Waterperry Gardens Limited
Incorporated: 21 March 1988 *Employees:* 78
Net Worth: £247,860 *Total Assets:* £600,026
Registered Office: Waterperry Horticultural Centre, Waterperry Gardens, Waterperry, Wheatley, Oxon, OX33 1JZ
Parent: The Fellowship of The School of Economic Science
Officers: Simon Nicholas Buchanan [1966] Director/Sculptor; Avril Cairncross [1951] Director/Retired Teacher; Clive Reginald Meek [1963] Director/Investment Management; Geoffrey Neville Pearce [1938] Director/Accountant

Watt (W) Ltd
Incorporated: 2 January 2019
Registered Office: 53 Chancellor House, 395 Rotherhithe New Road, London, SE16 3FP
Shareholders: Ka Yi Li; Bogdan Culda
Officers: Bogdan Culda [1993] Director/Engineer [Romanian]; Ka Yi Li [1994] Director/Consultant [Hong Kong]

Wellbeing and Balance Limited
Incorporated: 1 August 2018
Registered Office: 9 Mafeking Road, Enfield, Middlesex, EN1 3SS
Major Shareholder: Georgina Casely Hayford Awuku
Officers: Georgina Casely Hayford Awuku [1977] Director/Nurse [Ghanaian]

What's Good Limited
Incorporated: 10 November 2014
Registered Office: 70 Meadow Waye, London, TW5 9EZ
Major Shareholder: Mohammad Idrees Rasouli
Officers: Mohammad Idrees Rasouli [1986] Director/Innovation Design Engineer

Who Knows Limited
Incorporated: 7 September 2010
Net Worth: £220 *Total Assets:* £60,582
Registered Office: 62 Waverley Crescent, Cumbernauld, N Lanarks, G67 4BG
Major Shareholder: Tracy Scott
Officers: Douglas Kay Scott [1967] Director; Tracy Scott [1967] Director

Wilanow:Import Export Ltd
Incorporated: 11 October 2018
Registered Office: 27 Old Gloucester Street, London, WC1N 3AX
Officers: Khaled Djouaher [1981] Director/Manager Import Export [Polish]

Wild Cane Ltd.
Incorporated: 6 December 2017
Registered Office: 4 Brockwell Avenue, Beckenham, Kent, BR3 3GF
Major Shareholder: Ramzi Issa
Officers: Ramzi Issa [1989] Director/Founder

The Wise Herb Company Limited
Incorporated: 19 December 2017
Registered Office: 12 Dewe Lane, Burghfield, Reading, Berks, RG30 3SU
Major Shareholder: Ketan Harshad Joshi
Officers: Carolynne Yew Kiew Joshi [1959] Director; Dev Ketan Kong Joshi [1994] Director; Jay Ketan Kong Joshi [1992] Director; Dr Ketan Harshad Joshi [1961] Director

Wonky Food Limited
Incorporated: 12 January 2015
Net Worth: £3 *Total Assets:* £3
Registered Office: 41 Akeman Street, Combe, Witney, Oxon, OX29 8NZ
Shareholders: Ashley Helen Cavers; John Carl Cavers; Laura Isabel Snook
Officers: Ashley Helen Cavers [1973] Director/Researcher; John Carl Cavers [1978] Director/Web Developer [British/American]; Laura Isabel Snook [1980] Director/Caterer

Wonky Group Ltd
Incorporated: 10 August 2017
Registered Office: 41 Akeman Street, Combe, Witney, Oxon, OX29 8NZ
Parent: Wonky Food Limited
Officers: Ashley Helen Cavers [1973] Director/Researcher; Joseph Cottingham [1973] Director of Fresh Produce Company; Dr Edward Donald Berkerley Gray [1984] Director of Fresh Produce Company; Laura Isabel Snook [1980] Director/Caterer

Woolfies Ltd
Incorporated: 13 August 2018
Registered Office: Sutton House, Howard Street, Gloucester, GL1 4UR
Major Shareholder: Daniel Joseph Woolf
Officers: Daniel Joseph Woolf [1984] Director/Actor

F. A. Young Farm Produce Limited
Incorporated: 13 March 2007 *Employees:* 11
Net Worth: £521,318 *Total Assets:* £647,309
Registered Office: Hayeswood Farm, Hayeswood Road, Timsbury, Bath, BA2 0FQ
Shareholders: Mary Elizabeth Young; Priscilla Elaine Young
Officers: Melanie Elizabeth Davies [1963] Director/Manager; Priscilla Elaine Young [1940] Director/Entrepreneur

Zendegii Frill Limited
Incorporated: 21 March 2014 *Employees:* 9
Net Worth: £35,786 *Total Assets:* £256,393
Registered Office: Unit 10, 10 Acklam Road, London, W10 5QZ
Major Shareholder: Khosro Ezaz-Nikpay
Officers: Dr Khosro Ezaz-Nikpay [1965] Director [German]; Anna Stina Sjostrom Eriksson [1971] Director/Country Manager [Swedish]

Zendegii Retail Limited
Incorporated: 12 December 2012
Net Worth: £10,137 *Total Assets:* £339,792
Registered Office: Unit 10, 10 Acklam Road, London, W10 5QZ
Shareholders: Khosro Ezaz-Nikpay; Khosro Ezaz-Nikpay
Officers: Fatemeh Vasheghani Farahani, Secretary; Dr Khosro Ezaz-Nikpay [1965] Director [German]; Peter Malcolm Lowthian Freedman [1956] Director/Consultant

Zion Kitchen Limited
Incorporated: 10 January 2012
Registered Office: 4 Merridale, Carston Close, Lee Green, London, SE12 8TG
Major Shareholder: Constance Okyere-Buor
Officers: Constance Okyere-Buor [1956] Director

Zip & Zing Juices Ltd
Incorporated: 13 January 2016
Net Worth: £2,676 *Total Assets:* £2,676
Registered Office: Flat 9, 195 Long Lane, London, SE1 4PD
Major Shareholder: Antony Ian Cervantes
Officers: Antony Ian Cervantes [1971] Director

Index of Directorships

Abay, Ilhan
Juices on the Go Ltd

Abdalla, Abdalla Hussain
Suda Green REV Investment Ltd

Abdulrahman, Lulwa
The Good MLK Ltd

Abdurasul, Shamagdiev
UK Dorset Ltd

Ackerman, Nicholas Leigh
One54 Holdings Ltd

Acock, Philip John
My Goodness (British Farmers) Ltd

Adeniyi, Sunday
Trim and Trendy Limited

Adeosun, Adebayo
Anglo African Food & Beverages Holding

Adnan, Ali
Mebifarm Ltd

Adzofu, Benjamin
Dzatafia Ltd

Ageba, David Msughter
Purity Organic Juice Ltd

Agyeman, Abena
Odopa Foods Ltd

Ahmad, Rafiq
Rafiq Costcutter Limited

Aiyewumi, Adeyemi
Golden Hibiscus Foods and Drinks Ltd

Aiyewumi, Steven
Golden Hibiscus Foods and Drinks Ltd

Ajose, Emmanuel
FruitFullFruits Ltd

Akeroyd, Annabel Charlotte
Realdrink Ltd

Akeroyd, Simon Andrew
Realdrink Ltd

Akinrinlude, Marie-Olive
Borderless Catering Ltd

Ali, Ayesha
Nourish Juice Ltd

Ali, Liaqat
Ariana Foods (PVT) Ltd

Ali, Sharmarke Haydar
Ammo Your Ammunition to Greatness

Archard, Paul
The Refreshing Drinks Co Ltd

Archer, Ross
Smoofeez Limited

Audu, Paul Abdul-Abbass
Chocquers Limited

Awada, Houssein
AWA Nature Ltd

Awuku, Georgina Casely Hayford
Wellbeing and Balance Limited

Ayadi, Youssri
Ayad Corporation Ltd

Bacon, Henry Hickman
One54 Holdings Ltd

Baidoo, Giuseppe
Ethically Made Ltd
Lemony Drinks Ltd

Baker, Philip William
Onion Jo Limited

Barnes, Richard Julian
Clearly Juice Limited

Barnes, Sally
Clearly Juice Limited

Barrow, Jordan
Fitness Fruits Limited

Barry, Kevin Paul
Fresh Manchester Ltd

Baxter, Audrey Caroline
Baxters Food Group Limited

Beckles, Colin
Demcar UK Limited

Beckles, Simone
Demcar UK Limited

Bedi, Aneil
The Refreshing Drinks Co Ltd

Belch, Gordon James
Strive Products Sco Limited

Benson, Alexia Louise
Bensons Fruit Juice Limited

Benson, Jeremy
Bensons Fruit Juice Limited

Blackwood, Silbert
Nattyroots Ital Juice Limited

Boglione, Harry Luca
Gilt & Flint Ltd

Bolarin, Yetunde Folasade
Adunni Foods Ltd

Bolarinwa, Ilerika Jamie Oluwayomi
The Vitsuk Ltd

Bowers, Michael David
Little Stour Orchard Ltd

Bowers, Sarah Jane, Dr
Little Stour Orchard Ltd

Boye Doe, Andrew Adinorte
One54 Holdings Ltd

Boyle, Gregory Thomas
Good Natured (Happy Monkey) Ltd

Bradley, Elizabeth Madeleine
Bradleys Juices Limited

Bradley, Jeffrey Charles Richard
Hidden Orchard Ltd

Bradley, John Miles
Bradleys Juices Limited

Bremner, Stuart John
The Juicing Co Ltd

Bremner, Vanessa Marianne
The Juicing Co Ltd

Browne, Daliah
Exclusively Unique Ltd

Buchanan, Simon Nicholas
Waterperry Gardens Limited

Buddhasingh, Carl
Anglo African Food & Beverages Holding

Burford, Michael
Rosehip Farms Limited

Burford, Rikki Alice, Dr
Rosehip Farms Limited

Burns, Matthew Patrick
Dnajuices Limited

Burris, Joseph
Bennu Rising Ltd.

Bustillo, Vita
Glotedragon Ltd

Buswell, Annette
Juice 1st Limited

Cafun, Natalie Marie-Colette
Juicyology Ltd

Cairncross, Avril
Waterperry Gardens Limited

Campbell, Amani
Ice N Creamz Limited

Campbell, Kirstie Eira
Seabuckthorn Scotland CIC

Camps, Lisa
The Naked Juice Co Ltd

Carpenter, Henry
Go Super You Limited

Castaneda, Javier
Spnet Ltd.

Castaneda, Miguel
Spnet Ltd.

Cavers, Ashley Helen
Wonky Food Limited
Wonky Group Ltd

Cavers, John Carl
Wonky Food Limited

Caws, Jacqueline
Dr. Chocolate Limited

Cervantes, Antony Ian
Zip & Zing Juices Ltd

Challinor, Lewis Dan
Bright Smoothies Ltd

Chan, Esther Phaik Khay
Alkalize Me Ltd

Channer, Lucy Conchita
Rootyfruit Limited

Cherquaoui, Yasmine
Ready Steady Glow London Ltd

Cherruault, Florence Agnes Coco
The Pickle House Limited

Chevallier Guild, Henry
H & D Ventures Limited

Chopra, Ritu
Ipure Nutrition Limited

Chowdhury, Jewel
Sweet Palm Ltd

Christiansson, Tua
Presse Limited

Clarke, Chardonay
Love Skin Co Ltd

Clavijo, Eduardo Jose
CCM Enterprises Limited

Clayton, James Oliver
Karma Juice Ltd

Clifford, Lara
Go Super You Limited

Cochrane, Robert Nathaniel
9 Pillars Ltd

Coelho, Priya
Tam Events & Cafe Ltd

Coker, Olrick
A2A Foods Limited

Coker, Siobhan
A2A Foods Limited

Colletti, Giuseppe
Tower Nursery Limited

Colville, James Alaric
Fruitful Durham CIC

Comyn, Charles David Courtney
One54 Holdings Ltd

Cook, Mark
CPJLondon Ltd

Cope, George Edward Brian
The Juice Tap Ltd

Copeland, Jourdan
The Holy Grain Co Ltd.

Cordi-Piec, Britt, Dr
Livewheatgrass Limited

Costa, Manuel Carlos Seara
Frol Explorer Ltd

Cottingham, Joseph
Wonky Group Ltd

Court, Stephen James
Crown of Life Juices Ltd

Covatariu, Claudia
The Dirty Milkshake Ltd

Cozzi, Antony Richard
Verjuice Limited

Cozzi, Carole May Guotavia
Verjuice Limited

Crawford, Kelly
Armagh Juice Co Ltd

Crossman, Benjamin Andrew
Ben Crossman Limited

Cserveni, Peter Zoltan
Natvitanet Ltd

Culda, Bogdan
Watt (W) Ltd

Cunningham, Carol
California Girl Foods Ltd

Daly, Christina
Islandgal Juice Ltd

Danquah, Joseph
Eye Adom Market Limited

Dattani, Rajesh
Perfect Brands (Europe) Ltd
Perfect Brands Ltd

Dattani, Sanjay
Perfect Brands Ltd
Perfect Brands (Europe) Ltd

Davenport, James Lewis
Fresh Trading Limited
Innocent Limited

Davies, Malcolm
J.C.Davies & Hall Limited

Davies, Melanie Elizabeth
F. A. Young Farm Produce Ltd

Davis, Ronald
Baxters Food Group Limited

De Bruin, Werner
Sprosen Accounts Ltd

Dede, Mahmut
Juice Junkie London Limited

Denayer, Paul
Alpro (UK) Limited

Devi, Jesvinder
Go Fresh Ltd

Dewan, MD Yasin
The Dirty Milkshake Ltd

Diamond, Leon Edward
Plenish Cleanse Ltd

Dixon, Angus Martin
Elgin's Orchard Ltd

Djouaher, Khaled
Wilanow:Import Export Ltd

Dobson, Jean Mary
TJ & PJ Dobson Ltd

Dobson, Philip John
TJ & PJ Dobson Ltd

Dobson, Thomas Jonathan
TJ & PJ Dobson Ltd
Fruit Smoothies Ltd

Donaldson, Iain
Judge Juice Ltd

Donker, Evert
Chiltern Ridge Apple Juice Ltd

Donovan, Stephen
Garden Press Ltd

Dowson, Sarah Mary Helen
Impressive Juices Ltd

Drain, John
JBC Juices Limited

Dry, Robert
Dboost Drinks Limited

Dry, Sharon
Dboost Drinks Limited

Duncan, Ruel Levi
Nattyroots Ital Juice Limited

Duraiz, Mohammad Amash
Chefs Food Products Ltd

Dyer, Daniel
Spider Cider Ltd

Edwards, Mike
Snowdonia Birch Water Ltd

El-Akiki, Charbel
Akiki Organics (UK) Limited

Elsayed Marghany, Karim Marghany
MG International Trading UK Ltd

Embrechts, Rinni
Umoba Ltd

Emery, Dannielle Lauren
Freshleigh Ltd

Enver, Osman
Bringing Eden Ltd

Evans, Michael John
H2T Food & Drink Limited

Ezaz-Nikpay, Khosro, Dr
Zendegii Frill Limited
Zendegii Retail Limited

Ezenekwe Jr, Chika Nnadozie Osamwonyi
Honestly Limited

Faes, Nikolaas Francois Joanna
Alba of Tonbridge Limited

Faes, Sarah Jane Parbery
Alba of Tonbridge Limited

Falconer, William Robert
One54 Holdings Ltd

Faltischek, Denise Menikheim
Orchard House Foods Limited

Farparan, Garry
Phoenexus Ltd

Fayyaz, Omar
Sunlife Organics Limited

Femi-Obasan, Enitan Adebola
Kleos Naturals Ltd

Fenton, Hannah Clare
Tiddly Pommes Ltd

Ferencz, Balazs
Barsupply Limited

Field, Andrew James Darragh
Razoo Limited

Field, Rosheeka Dilhani Amarasekara
Razoo Limited

Fisher, John James
BB & F Consultants Limited

Fitzpatrick, Daniel Paul
Gilt & Flint Ltd

Fletcher, Thomas
Rejuce Limited

Foottit, Geeta Ann
Juice Philosophy Limited

Ford, Peter James
Orchard Origins C.I.C.

Fordham, Christopher Michael Peter
Dean Press Cider Ltd.

Foster, Charles Bond
Felukka Limited

Foustok, Aida
Juicebaby Ltd.

France, Denis
Handmade Cider Co Ltd

Freedman, Peter Malcolm Lowthian
Zendegii Retail Limited

Galea, Simon David
The Refreshing Drinks Co Ltd

Gallagher, John Stephen
Ella Drinks Limited

Gazeley, Albert Edward
Coton Orchard Limited

Gazeley, Anna Teresa
Coton Orchard Limited

Gazeley, Supanee
Coton Orchard Limited

Ghani, Abeda Rashid
Juiceworks Limited

Ghani, Tariq Sultan
Juiceworks Limited

Ghuman, Haseeb
CPJLondon Ltd

Gibb, Andrew Donald Bruce
Coldpress Foods Limited

Gibb, Chloe Samantha
Coldpress Foods Limited

Godfrey, Julian Ashley
Fruitful Durham CIC

Godinet, Rachael
The Juice Warrior Ltd

Gonzalez, Mateo Akira Notsuke
Selva Group Limited

Gough, Edward Thomas
Direct Ingredients Limited
Ingredients Direct (UK) Ltd

Granozio, Roberto Nicholas
Seabuckthorn Scotland CIC

Gray, Edward Donald Berkerley, Dr
Wonky Group Ltd

Green, Laurence John
Orchard Origins C.I.C.

Griffin, Rupert Ivor James
Tiddly Pommes Ltd

Gueorguieva, Denitsa Valerieva
AMM Ventures Ltd

Haigh, Terence Richard James
AMC Freshly Squeezed (UK) Ltd

Hall, James
J.C.Davies & Hall Limited

Hamilton, Ian
Kunubu Ltd

Harahwa, Dumiso
LSG PVT Ltd

Harding, Sally
Truth Tonics Limited

Harrison, Antony Thomas, Lord
Garden House Farms Limited

Hashi, Abdihaking
H & R Partners Limited

Hawkins, James Dean
The Fruit and Veg Co Leeds Ltd

Helbling, Andrew Alistair
Duskin Farm Limited

Helbling, Susan Jane
Duskin Farm Limited

Helton, Kevin
Carbon Fresh Limited

Henry, Darren Mark
Juice Garden Limited

Hernandez, Rodrigo Guillermo Emilio
Ultimate Juice Limited

Hickling, Darren
Aero Cosmetics Limited

Hill, Emerson
Fresh Bagels Ltd.

Hill, Nikki
Oliviccio Ltd

Hillary, Lee Scott
The Frozen Cocktail Co Ltd

Hinds, Jordan Patrick
J.P Hinds Limited

Hobbs, Michael John
Inside Armour Ltd

Hofmann, Patrick Hamilkar
Sundance Partners Limited

Holder, Dunstan Godfrey
Funtime Products Limited

Holder, Yvette Anne
Funtime Products Limited

Holland, Graeme
Pura Pressed Ltd

House, Frances Bryony
The Cotswold Fruit Co Ltd.

Hurrell, Brian Peter Robert
Orchard Origins C.I.C.

Hutchison, Jane Erica
Carbon Fresh Limited

Ijuo, Eke
Clynes Farms Ltd

Ikpe-Adegwu, Joseph Ijuo
Clynes Farms Ltd

Imlach, Robert Francis
Liberty Orchards Limited

Irving, Simone Shushannah
Fruiture Ltd

Issa, Ramzi
Wild Cane Ltd.

Jabrane, Thomas Aymen, Dr
Livitus Limited

Jarvis, Andrew
Andrew M Jarvis Limited

Jervis, Monica Frances
Fruit International Limited

Joannides, Kyriacos
Asher & Son (Fruit & Vegetable Supplies)

Johansson, Namulindwa
Azalizo Foods Ltd

Johnson, Michelle
Real Shhh Limited

Johnson, Rhys
Crosby Beverages Ltd

Johnson, Sharon
Chocquers Limited

Jolly, Roger Melville
Gold Star Soft Drinks Westcountry Ltd

Jones, Raemonde
Direct Ingredients Limited
Ingredients Direct (UK) Ltd

Jordan, Damien Paul
Natural CBD Solutions Ltd

Joshi, Carolynne Yew Kiew
The Wise Herb Co Ltd

Joshi, Dev Ketan Kong
The Food and Drink Development Co Ltd
The Wise Herb Co Ltd

Joshi, Jay Ketan Kong
The Food and Drink Development Co Ltd
The Wise Herb Co Ltd

Joshi, Ketan Harshad, Dr
The Food and Drink Development Co Ltd
The Wise Herb Co Ltd

Karakoc, Ercumet
Juice and Vegan Ltd

Kasongo, Yohari
Neema Food Ltd

Kasprzak, Miroslaw Marek, Dr
Academic Fruits Limited

Keeble, Richard John
Stamford Juice Co Ltd

Kelly, Lorna Ruth
Seabuckthorn Scotland CIC

Khan, Asmatullah
Ariana Foods (PVT) Ltd

Khan, Mohammed Sobur
Prickly Pear Potion Ltd

Khan, Tusif
Bear Dough Limited

Khemdoudi, Mohamed Saber
Fruitfullest Ltd.

Kidane, Aron
The Juice Unit Ltd

Kim, Sonmi
Sundance Partners Limited

Komlosi, Sandor
Juice and Go Ltd

Konde, Yindula Bokolombe Emilie
Purity Organic Juice Ltd

Kovacs, Gabriella
Natvitanet Ltd

Kular, Akash Deep Singh
Coco Twist Ltd

Kurtz, Rachel May
Fruitful Durham CIC

Lameire, Daniel Jeffery
Route 33 Limited

Lamont, Douglas Ross
Fresh Trading Limited
Innocent Limited

Lamote, Sven
Alpro (UK) Limited

Langrock, James Michael
Orchard House Foods Limited

Ledger, Richard Dean
Sinful Foods Limited

Lee, Andrew John, Dr
Lytegro Limited

Lee, Buddy
Vegan Monster Ltd

Lemmey, Alison Jean
Liberty Orchards Limited

Lemmey, Peter John
Liberty Orchards Limited

Lester, Tulin
Pome de Vita Limited

Lethem, Aidan Julius
Doromomo & Sons Ltd

Li, Ka Yi
Watt (W) Ltd

Lin, Wan-Hsuan
Alkalize Me Ltd

Lindgren, David Richard
The Cotswold Fruit Co Ltd.

Little, Henry
JBC Juices Limited

Lucas, Max
Purer Ltd

Lynskey, Christine Sarah
Rose and Gold Drinks Limited

Lyte, Mark
Lytegro Limited

Mackintosh, Nicholas Ian MacDonald
Urban Juice Ltd

Madlala, Sphelo Sphephelo Skhumbuzo
The Oxford Juice Co Ltd

Maguire, Paula Michelle
Cowherds Juicery Limited

Maloney, Brian
Plenish Cleanse Ltd

Mam, Mary
SRAM & MRAM Limited
SRAM & MRAM Technologies and Resources

Maniscalco, Domenica
Tower Nursery Limited

Manziala, Alfred Musasa
Fimivita Agrimining Limited

Martin, Michael
Muscle in Motion Ltd

Martins, Rafael Alexandre Pires
Pastel D'Nata Ltd.

Masoud, Faisal
Cafe Tani Limited

Matheson, Roy
Elgin's Orchard Ltd

Matheson, Valerie Elizabeth
Elgin's Orchard Ltd

Maxfield, Darren
Health Hut NW Ltd

May, Joseph Piers Cecil
Passion 4 Juice Limited

McCarter, Andrew Donald
Hero Solutions Limited

McDonald, Rory
Naturally Ugly Ltd

McGill, Michael Scott
Baxters Food Group Limited

McPherson, Ryan James
McBerries Ltd

Meehan, Kevin Andrew
CCM Enterprises Limited

Meek, Clive Reginald
Waterperry Gardens Limited

Melville, Antony Richard David
Tiddly Pommes Ltd

Mengis, Verena
Straight Up Zesty Ltd.

Miah, Badrul
Bimim Foods Limited

Middleton, Phoebe
Desert Raw Ltd

Middleton, Sophie Ann
Raw Candy Ltd

Mir, Naila
Orchard Blossoms Limited

Mir, Sierra
Orchard Blossoms Limited

Mir, Tabassum
Orchard Blossoms Limited

Mohajerani, Hoda
Chakra Chai Limited

Moore, Benjamin
Health Hut NW Ltd

Moorhead, Patrick Jonathan Joseph
Brew Crew & Co. Limited

Morais, John Anthony Pinto
Claense Ltd

Morant, Leon David
Get Juiced Tooting Ltd

Morland, Victoria
Liberty Orchards Limited

Morris, Melissa Michelle
Pressed Ltd

Mosley, Chris
Garden Press Ltd

Mosley, Kate Frances
Garden Press Ltd

Moulding, Jamie
Grace Under Pressure Ltd

Moulding, Jessica Mary
Grace Under Pressure Ltd

Muneer, Muhammad
Elmsfield Enterprises Limited

Murgatroyd, Paula Melinda
Impressive Juices Ltd

Naeem, Abdul
Get Fresh Ltd

Neacsu, Ovidiu
Neacsu Construct Ltd

Neilson, Louise Beverley, Dr
H2T Food & Drink Limited

O'Neill, Amy
Juicee Beets Ltd

Oakes, Kelly
The Good Juice Co Ltd

Obi, Emmanuel Chinonye
Mobie Corporation Limited

Odame-Labi, Elizabeth
ABA Foods Limited

Odame-Labi, Paula
ABA Foods Limited

Odeniyi, Laide
Hunterworth Ltd

Okos, Andrea Agota
Love Yourself UK Limited

Okpapi, John Ikhaobomhe
Endurance Juice Co Ltd

Okpapi, Michael Osizimhete
Endurance Juice Co Ltd

Okyere-Buor, Constance
Zion Kitchen Limited

Olali, Odi
Crosby Beverages Ltd

Olaoye, Oyedele Abidemi
Livitus Limited

Olusi, Olumolawa Oludotun
Iorange UK Limited

Onuh, Michael Cornerstone
J.T Freshly Limited

Opoku, Henrietta
Eye Adom Market Limited

Otokiti, Olayinka Ayodele
Greenie's Smoothies Limited

Owen, Samuel
My Monkey Doesn't Like Bananas Anymore

Owens, Brian
Rhythm Health Limited

Ozsumer, Taner
The Refreshing Drinks Co Ltd

Pane, Christopher
Revive Us Limited

Panesar, Parminder
Juice A Day Limited

Parffrey, Andrew
Suppers Ready Limited

Parvin, Dolly
BSP Juice Ltd

Paurache, Karrman Patience
Karrmancooks Ltd

Pearce, Geoffrey Neville
Waterperry Gardens Limited

Pearson, Emily, Honourable
Cowdray Live Ltd.

Pellegrino, Yves
Alpro (UK) Limited

Peng, Jiang
Hainan Super Industrial Ltd

Pietkiewicz, Marta
Martina Peters Ltd

Pike, Sally Jane
Orchard Origins C.I.C.

Pinnock, Peter Gavin
Kunubu Ltd

Pole, Erica Emily Eva
Route 33 Limited

Pole, Warren Douglas
Route 33 Limited

Potiwal, Neelam Wanti
Juiced Ltd

Potter, Rebecca
Truth Tonics Limited

Powell, Michael
Abanability Ltd

Pringle, Natalee
That Healthy Way Limited

Pringle, Norman Murray, Sir
Food Development Co Ltd

Qasim, Abaidullah
Get Juiced (UK) Ltd

Randhawa, Davinder Kaur
Sunrise Produce Ltd

Randhawa, Kuldip Singh
Sunrise Produce Ltd

Rasouli, Mohammad Idrees
What's Good Limited

Rayner, Philip John
Rayner and Rooster Limited

Rayner, Rebecca Eve
Rayner and Rooster Limited

Redman, Wayne
The Naked Juice Co Ltd

Richardson, Yusuf Ekow Obi
H & R Partners Limited

Robertson, Jordan
Pure Press Ltd

Robson, Peter
The Drinks Group Holdings Ltd

Roche, Scott Edward
Fresh Trading Limited
Innocent Limited

Rooke, Andrew James
Fruitapeel (Juice) Ltd

Rosen, Kara
Plenish Cleanse Ltd

Rowland, Phillip
The Frozen Cocktail Co Ltd

Rudge, Mark Andrew
Wasted Apple Co Ltd

Sadauskas, Antanas
Neptune SA Ltd

Sak, Robert Marek
Rawness Limited

Schiller, Mark Lawrence
Orchard House Foods Limited

Schoomhoven, Rajimi
Beermats4u Limited

Schoonhoven, Lukinus
Beermats4u Limited

Scott, Douglas Kay
Who Knows Limited

Scott, Tracy
Who Knows Limited

Seetharaman, Balasubramanian
SRAM & MRAM Limited
SRAM & MRAM Technologies and Resources

Selvi, Erdinc
Olives Britannia Foreign Trade Co. Ltd

Shah, Ali Hussain
Green-Beam Life Limited

Shah, Zayd Hussain
Green-Beam Life Limited

Shepherd-Smyth, Jon
Cowherds Juicery Limited

Shepherdson, Amy Victoria
Garden Press Ltd

Simpson, Olivia Rochelle
Jamcan Ltd

Sinera, Isatou
Healthy Drinks & Smoothie Ltd

Singhal, Raj
PG Foods Ltd

Sjostrom Eriksson, Anna Stina
Zendegii Frill Limited

Skidmore, Robin James
Orchard House Foods Limited

Slade, Jason Samuel
Gilt & Flint Ltd

Slootweg, Caroline
Rootyfruit Limited

Smedley, Pamela Ann
Four Elms Fruit Farm Limited

Smedley, Richard John
Four Elms Fruit Farm Limited
Four Elms Juice Limited

Smedley, Susan Jane
Four Elms Fruit Farm Limited
Four Elms Juice Limited

Smith, Benjamin David
Thornton Nurseries Ltd

Smith, David John
Thornton Nurseries Ltd

Smith, Graham Francis
The Juice Smith Limited

Smith, John William
Thornton Nurseries Ltd

Smith-Bernal, Richard
The Juice Smith Limited

Snook, Laura Isabel
Wonky Food Limited
Wonky Group Ltd

Sorken, Terje
Aspire Better Health Limited

Soroka, Ewa Stanislawa
Frugo Smoothies Ltd
E & M Soroka Ltd

Soroka, Michal
Frugo Smoothies Ltd
E & M Soroka Ltd

Sparrow, Miriam Hazel
PAS Engineering Limited

Sparrow, Paul Anthony
PAS Engineering Limited

Spencer, Harrison James
Juice A Day Limited

Staples, Ben Callum
Raw Cure Limited

Steltenpohl, Greg
Califia Farms UK Limited

Stevenson, Timothy Vernon King
CPRESS One Limited

Steward, David John
H & D Ventures Limited

Street, Jordan Karl
The Proper Protein Co Ltd.

Stutter, Denise
Juice Freaks Co Ltd

Summers, Jordan Blake
Earthstrong Juicery Ltd

Szymanski, Damian
Agro Plus Limited

Taheri, Ahmad Mansoor
Afgdryfruites.co.uk Limited

Talikowski, Krzysztof Stefan
Juice Delivery Service Ltd

Tayler, Janet Mary
Fruitful Durham CIC

Taylor, George Stanley James
JBC Juices Limited

Taylor, Martin John
Fresh Appeal Limited

Ter Laak, Anouk
SVZ (UK) Limited

Thomas, Katie Ann
Juice HQ Ltd

Thomas, Scott Jason
Juice HQ Ltd

Thomas, Silvia
Berrybegood Ltd

Thompson, Dwayne
Kemetic Cooks Ltd

Thompson, Edward Ballard
Pixley Berries (Juice) Limited

Thompson, Jermaine
Juice Junkiez Limited

Thompson, Paulette
Bare Goodness Limited

Thomson, Anne
Ella Drinks Limited

Tiglao, Ailyn
Frozenbeep Ltd

Tobin, Patrick James
Rhythm Health Limited

Tony-Uzoebo, Emeraba Afaoma
Trove International Limited

Toreki, Vince Mate
Barsupply Limited

Torres Ledezma, Cesar Enrique
Devon Garden Foods Limited

Trenkov, Nikolay Blagoev
Amaze Offers Ltd

Troughton, Helen
Armagh Juice Co Ltd

Troughton, Mark
Armagh Juice Co Ltd

Troughton, Philip
Armagh Juice Co Ltd

Tucker, Patricia Margaret
Passion 4 Juice Limited

Tunnicliff, Cy
Juice Fit JQ Limited

Turnbull, James Wilson
Food Development Co Ltd

Udeze, Daisy
Degarnix Ltd

Uffort, Eno William
Affybale Ltd

Uffort-Otuyelu, Affiong
Affybale Ltd

Ullah, Hafeez
Ariana Foods (PVT) Ltd

Van Der Snel-Nooteboom, Gerritje
Gerries Fruit Limited

Van Harn, Jules
Healthy Thirst Drinks Limited

Van Ooijen, Frank Christoffel
Healthy Thirst Drinks Limited

Van-Dongen, Michael
Vegishake Ltd

Wallis, Christopher Geden
Elmsfield Enterprises Limited

Walsh, Anthony
AW Consultancy & Solutions Ltd

Ward, Adam Silvanus
Never Not Natural Ltd

Ward, Regina Ann Elizabeth
Chakra Shots Limited

Web, Renell Hope
FruitFullFruits Ltd

Webb, Junior
DrJuicy Ltd

Webb, Lancelot Clive
DrJuicy Ltd

Wheeler, Glenn
Smartervites Ltd

Whewell, James Robert
Little Teapot Ltd

Wickens, Gary Christopher
W & W Drinks Ltd

Wilcox, Adrian
Orchard Origins C.I.C.

Wild, James Ainsley
Bear & Organics Limited

Willcox, Joanne
Restore Juice Co Ltd

Williams, Alexandra Frances
The Juice Executive Ltd

Williams-McKean, Kendal Elizabeth
Restore Juice Co Ltd

Willis, Shirley Ann
Benburb Bramleys Limited

Willis, Thomas David
Benburb Bramleys Limited

Wilson, Caroline
Devon Orchard Ltd

Wilson, Dawn
The Cane Press Ltd

Wilson, Martin Geoffrey
Devon Orchard Ltd

Wolfson, Andrew Daniel
Plenish Cleanse Ltd

Woodall, Guy, Dr
Healthy Thirst Drinks Limited

Woodall, Sheila Catherine
Healthy Thirst Drinks Limited

Woodhead, Carl
Oliviccio Ltd

Woolf, Daniel Joseph
Woolfies Ltd

Worrall, Richard Stuart
Hibitala UK Limited

Worth, Duncan Richard
Fresh Appeal Limited

Wyatt, Richard Anthony
W & W Drinks Ltd

Yasin, Mohammed Saleem
Hijama Ruqya Remedies Ltd

Yntema, Yde Bouke
Analytical-Solutions UK Ltd

Yombo-Djema, Rose Mauwa
Neema Food Ltd

Young, Cynthia Patricia
Rejuveu Ltd

Young, Priscilla Elaine
F. A. Young Farm Produce Ltd

Standard Industrial Classification
excluding
Manufacture of fruit and vegetable juice

01130 Growing of vegetables and melons, roots and tubers
Go Fresh Ltd
Mebifarm Ltd

01190 Growing of other non-perennial crops
Kunubu Ltd

01240 Growing of pome fruits and stone fruits
Analytical-Solutions UK Ltd
Coton Orchard Limited
Liberty Orchards Limited
Little Stour Orchard Ltd
Waterperry Gardens Limited

01280 Growing of spices, aromatic, drug and pharmaceutical crops
Dzatafia Ltd

01290 Growing of other perennial crops
Waterperry Gardens Limited

01490 Raising of other animals
Honestly Limited

01500 Mixed farming
Duskin Farm Limited
SRAM & MRAM Limited
SRAM & MRAM Technologies and Resources

01630 Post-harvest crop activities
Kunubu Ltd

02300 Gathering of wild growing non-wood products
Seabuckthorn Scotland CIC

09900 Support activities for other mining and quarrying
Fimivita Agrimining Limited
SRAM & MRAM Limited
SRAM & MRAM Technologies and Resources

10130 Production of meat and poultry meat products
PG Foods Ltd
Wilanow:Import Export Ltd

10310 Processing and preserving of potatoes
Ayad Corporation Ltd

10390 Other processing and preserving of fruit and vegetables [30]
Ammo Your Ammunition to Greatness
Asher & Son (Fruit & Vegetable Supplies)
Ayad Corporation Ltd
Baxters Food Group Limited
Ben Crossman Limited
Degarnix Ltd
Devon Garden Foods Limited
Ethically Made Ltd
Food Development Co Ltd
Fresh Trading Limited
Frol Explorer Ltd
Fruitful Durham CIC
H2T Food & Drink Limited
Innocent Limited
Lemony Drinks Ltd
MG International Trading UK Ltd
Naturally Ugly Ltd
Natvitanet Ltd
Odopa Foods Ltd
Pixley Berries (Juice) Limited
Presse Limited
Rawness Limited
Rayner and Rooster Limited
Razoo Limited
Refreshing Drinks Co Ltd
Tiddly Pommes Ltd
Vegan Monster Ltd
Wonky Food Limited
Wonky Group Ltd
F. A. Young Farm Produce Ltd

10410 Manufacture of oils and fats
Ayad Corporation Ltd
Chefs Food Products Ltd
Kleos Naturals Ltd

10420 Manufacture of margarine and similar edible fats
Degarnix Ltd

10511 Liquid milk and cream production
Alpro (UK) Limited
Chakra Chai Limited
Wilanow:Import Export Ltd

10519 Manufacture of other milk products
Alpro (UK) Limited
Chakra Chai Limited
Ben Crossman Limited
Dboost Drinks Limited
Doromomo & Sons Ltd
Food and Drink Development Co Ltd
Wise Herb Co Ltd

10520 Manufacture of ice cream
PG Foods Ltd
Perfect Brands (Europe) Ltd
Perfect Brands Ltd
Sprosen Accounts Ltd

10612 Manufacture of breakfast cereals and cereals-based food
PG Foods Ltd
Perfect Brands (Europe) Ltd
Perfect Brands Ltd

10710 Manufacture of bread; manufacture of fresh pastry goods and cakes
Fresh Bagels Ltd.
Holy Grain Co Ltd
Pastel D'Nata Ltd.
Raw Candy Ltd
Sprosen Accounts Ltd
Zion Kitchen Limited

10720 Manufacture of rusks and biscuits; manufacture of preserved pastry goods and cakes
Perfect Brands Ltd
Proper Protein Co Ltd.
Sprosen Accounts Ltd

10730 Manufacture of macaroni, noodles, couscous and similar farinaceous products
Ice N Creamz Limited

10810 Manufacture of sugar
Suda Green REV Investment Ltd

10821 Manufacture of cocoa and chocolate confectionery
Chocquers Limited
Desert Raw Ltd
Perfect Brands (Europe) Ltd
Raw Candy Ltd
Wilanow:Import Export Ltd

10822 Manufacture of sugar confectionery
Rootyfruit Limited

10831 Tea processing
H2T Food & Drink Limited
Juice Unit Ltd
Wise Herb Co Ltd

10832 Production of coffee and coffee substitutes
Brew Crew & Co. Limited
Califia Farms UK Limited

10840 Manufacture of condiments and seasonings
Azalizo Foods Ltd
Borderless Catering Ltd
Handmade Cider Co Ltd
Kemetic Cooks Ltd
Neema Food Ltd
Wonky Food Limited
Wonky Group Ltd

10850 Manufacture of prepared meals and dishes [13]
9 Pillars Ltd
Adunni Foods Ltd
Azalizo Foods Ltd
Baxters Food Group Limited
CPRESS One Limited
Food and Drink Development Co Ltd
Golden Hibiscus Foods and Drinks Ltd
J.P Hinds Limited
Ice N Creamz Limited
Juicee Beets Ltd
Pure Press Ltd
Ready Steady Glow London Ltd
Zion Kitchen Limited

The UK Juice Industry   dellam

10860 Manufacture of homogenized food preparations and dietetic food
Alpro (UK) Limited
Eye Adom Market Limited
Health Hut NW Ltd
Honestly Limited
Never Not Natural Ltd

10890 Manufacture of other food products n.e.c. [25]
9 Pillars Ltd
Affybale Ltd
Avobravo Limited
Baxters Food Group Limited
Bimim Foods Limited
Degarnix Ltd
Demcar UK Limited
Desert Raw Ltd
Devon Garden Foods Limited
Eye Adom Market Limited
H2T Food & Drink Limited
Ice N Creamz Limited
Innocent Limited
Kemetic Cooks Ltd
MG International Trading UK Ltd
Nourish Juice Ltd
Odopa Foods Ltd
Olives Britannia Foreign Trade Co. Ltd
Presse Limited
Proper Protein Co Ltd.
Real Shhh Limited
Refreshing Drinks Co Ltd
Revive Us Limited
Wonky Food Limited
Wonky Group Ltd

11010 Distilling, rectifying and blending of spirits
Food Development Co Ltd
Liberty Orchards Limited
Neptune SA Ltd
Spnet Ltd.
UK Dorset Ltd

11030 Manufacture of cider and other fruit wines [14]
Analytical-Solutions UK Ltd
Bensons Fruit Juice Limited
Cotswold Fruit Co Ltd.
Crosby Beverages Ltd
Dean Press Cider Ltd.
Handmade Cider Co Ltd
Hidden Orchard Ltd
Liberty Orchards Limited
Little Teapot Ltd
Neptune SA Ltd
Orchard Origins C.I.C.
Tiddly Pommes Ltd
W & W Drinks Ltd
Wasted Apple Co Ltd

11040 Manufacture of other non-distilled fermented beverages
Anglo African Food & Beverages Holding
Juiceworks Limited
Presse Limited

11050 Manufacture of beer
Crosby Beverages Ltd
Doromomo & Sons Ltd
Gilt & Flint Ltd
Little Teapot Ltd
W & W Drinks Ltd

11070 Manufacture of soft drinks; production of mineral waters and other bottled waters [27]
Ammo Your Ammunition to Greatness
Anglo African Food & Beverages Holding
Armagh Juice Co Ltd
Avobravo Limited
Bennu Rising Ltd.
Bright Smoothies Ltd
Chakra Chai Limited
Chocquers Limited
Crosby Beverages Ltd
Drinks Group Holdings Ltd
Ella Drinks Limited
Endurance Juice Co Ltd
Food and Drink Development Co Ltd
Grace Under Pressure Ltd
Handmade Cider Co Ltd
Healthy Thirst Drinks Limited
Hidden Orchard Ltd
Kemetic Cooks Ltd
Livitus Limited
Neptune SA Ltd
Oxford Juice Co Ltd
Plenish Cleanse Ltd
Razoo Limited
Refreshing Drinks Co Ltd
Trove International Limited
UK Dorset Ltd
Wise Herb Co Ltd

13990 Manufacture of other textiles n.e.c.
Olives Britannia Foreign Trade Co. Ltd

20411 Manufacture of soap and detergents
Kleos Naturals Ltd

20530 Manufacture of essential oils
Chefs Food Products Ltd

20590 Manufacture of other chemical products n.e.c.
Doromomo & Sons Ltd
Lytegro Limited

21100 Manufacture of basic pharmaceutical products
Revive Us Limited

32990 Other manufacturing n.e.c.
Ariana Foods (PVT) Ltd

36000 Water collection, treatment and supply
Elmsfield Enterprises Limited

39000 Remediation activities and other waste management services
Smoofeez Limited

43390 Other building completion and finishing
Elmsfield Enterprises Limited

46110 Agents selling agricultural raw materials, livestock, textile raw materials and semi-finished goods
LSG PVT Ltd

46210 Wholesale of grain, unmanufactured tobacco, seeds and animal feeds
MG International Trading UK Ltd

46310 Wholesale of fruit and vegetables
Fruitfullest Ltd.
Mebifarm Ltd
Sweet Palm Ltd

46341 Wholesale of fruit and vegetable juices, mineral water and soft drinks [16]
AWA Nature Ltd
Bennu Rising Ltd.
Bright Smoothies Ltd
CCM Enterprises Limited
Cane Press Ltd
J.C.Davies & Hall Limited
Fruitfullest Ltd.
Go Fresh Ltd
Gold Star Soft Drinks Westcountry Ltd
Juice Junkie London Limited
Juice Junkiez Limited
Juice Warrior Ltd
McBerries Ltd
Pixley Berries (Juice) Limited
Rejuveu Ltd
Route 33 Limited

46380 Wholesale of other food, including fish, crustaceans and molluscs
Honestly Limited

46390 Non-specialised wholesale of food, beverages and tobacco
Bimim Foods Limited
Chefs Food Products Ltd

46690 Wholesale of other machinery and equipment
Mebifarm Ltd

46760 Wholesale of other intermediate products
CPJLondon Ltd

46900 Non-specialised wholesale trade
Aero Cosmetics Limited
Amaze Offers Ltd
CPJLondon Ltd
Olives Britannia Foreign Trade Co. Ltd
Spnet Ltd.

47110 Retail sale in non-specialised stores with food, beverages or tobacco predominating
J.P Hinds Limited
Revive Us Limited

47210 Retail sale of fruit and vegetables in specialised stores
Asher & Son (Fruit & Vegetable Supplies)
Fruitfullest Ltd.
Sweet Palm Ltd

47250 Retail sale of beverages in specialised stores
Bringing Eden Ltd
Pure Press Ltd

47290 Other retail sale of food in specialised stores
Bringing Eden Ltd
Juicebaby Ltd.
Oliviccio Ltd

47510 Retail sale of textiles in specialised stores
Mobie Corporation Limited

47710 Retail sale of clothing in specialised stores
Woolfies Ltd

47750 Retail sale of cosmetic and toilet articles in specialised stores
Kleos Naturals Ltd
Love Skin Co Ltd

47760 Retail sale of flowers, plants, seeds, fertilizers, pet animals and pet food in specialised stores
Rosehip Farms Limited
Waterperry Gardens Limited

47810 Retail sale via stalls and markets of food, beverages and tobacco products
Bright Smoothies Ltd
Crown of Life Juices Ltd
Go Fresh Ltd
Watt (W) Ltd

47910 Retail sale via mail order houses or via Internet
Kunubu Ltd
Natvitanet Ltd

47990 Other retail sale not in stores, stalls or markets
Watt (W) Ltd

55209 Other holiday and other collective accommodation
Juice Delivery Service Ltd

56101 Licenced restaurants
Smoofeez Limited

56102 Unlicenced restaurants and cafes
Brew Crew & Co. Limited

56103 Take-away food shops and mobile food stands
Chocquers Limited
Claense Ltd
Naturally Ugly Ltd
Pastel D'Nata Ltd.
Pure Press Ltd
Real Shhh Limited

56210 Event catering activities
Azalizo Foods Ltd
Borderless Catering Ltd
Naturally Ugly Ltd
Passion 4 Juice Limited

56290 Other food services
Borderless Catering Ltd
Dirty Milkshake Ltd
Livitus Limited
Odopa Foods Ltd
Pastel D'Nata Ltd.
Rosehip Farms Limited

59112 Video production activities
Martina Peters Ltd

59113 Television programme production activities
Coco Twist Ltd

61200 Wireless telecommunications activities
Spnet Ltd.

62012 Business and domestic software development
Hero Solutions Limited
SRAM & MRAM Limited
SRAM & MRAM Technologies and Resources

62020 Information technology consultancy activities
Hero Solutions Limited

63120 Web portals
Martina Peters Ltd

64209 Activities of other holding companies n.e.c.
One54 Holdings Ltd

64306 Activities of real estate investment trusts
Hainan Super Industrial Ltd

68201 Renting and operating of Housing Association real estate
TJ & PJ Dobson Ltd

70100 Activities of head offices
Food Development Co Ltd

70229 Management consultancy activities other than financial management
Analytical-Solutions UK Ltd
Frol Explorer Ltd
Hunterworth Ltd
Trim and Trendy Limited

71111 Architectural activities
Suda Green REV Investment Ltd

72190 Other research and experimental development on natural sciences and engineering
Elmsfield Enterprises Limited

79909 Other reservation service activities n.e.c.
Ready Steady Glow London Ltd

81210 General cleaning of buildings
Amaze Offers Ltd
Martina Peters Ltd

86900 Other human health activities
Demcar UK Limited
Dzatafia Ltd
Love Yourself UK Limited
Smoofeez Limited

93130 Fitness facilities
Ready Steady Glow London Ltd

93199 Other sports activities
Claense Ltd
Coco Twist Ltd

96020 Hairdressing and other beauty treatment
Amaze Offers Ltd
Exclusively Unique Ltd

96040 Physical well-being activities
Claense Ltd
Raw Candy Ltd
Real Shhh Limited

96090 Other service activities n.e.c.
LSG PVT Ltd
Orchard Origins C.I.C.

Printed in 8pt Nimbus Sans L

Designed by URW++ Design and Development GmbH

Dellam Publishing Limited

2 Heath Drive, Sutton, Surrey, SM2 5RP

Fax: 020 8770 7478   email: enquiries@dellam.com

SAN: 0177881   EAN/GLN: 5030670177882

www.ingramcontent.com/pod-product-compliance
Lightning Source LLC
Chambersburg PA
CBHW081128080526
44587CB00021B/3797